A SHORT

OF THE

MOST ESSENTIAL POINTS
IN
HAWAIIAN GRAMMAR

A SHORT SYNOPSIS
OF THE
MOST ESSENTIAL POINTS
IN
HAWAIIAN
GRAMMAR

BY
W. D. ALEXANDER

CHARLES E. TUTTLE COMPANY
Rutland, Vermont & Tokyo, Japan

Representatives
Continental Europe: BOXERBOOKS, INC., *Zurich*
British Isles: PRENTICE-HALL INTERNATIONAL, INC., *London*
Australasia: PAUL FLESCH & CO., PTY. LTD., *Melbourne*
Canada: HURTIG PUBLISHERS, *Edmonton*

Published by the Charles E. Tuttle Company, Inc.
of Rutland, Vermont & Tokyo, Japan
with editorial offices at
Suido 1-chome, 2-6, Bunkyo-ku, Tokyo, Japan

Copyright in Japan, 1968, by Charles E. Tuttle Co., Inc.

Library of Congress Catalog Card No. 68-13866

International Standard Book No. 0-8048-0528-8

First Tuttle edition, 1968
Fourth printing, 1975

PRINTED IN JAPAN

PUBLISHER'S FOREWORD

LEARNING the language of the native Hawaiians was only one of the problems that faced the original band of missionaries who arrived in March, 1820, on the shores of the then-called Sandwich Islands. Having survived the rigors of their 18,000-mile, five-month ocean voyage from Boston, and finally having gained the permission of King Kamehameha II to remain in the islands on probation for a year, the dedicated young Christians set about overcoming the language barrier with typical determination and fortitude.

It was not long before they detected 20,000 words in the Hawaiian vocabulary and commenced to establish for the first time a conversion of these words into written form. From there, further and more complicated studies were made of the "Hawaiian branch of the Polynesian language."

The current synopsis of Hawaiian grammar was last published in 1924 (in a revised fifth edition). It was first published by missionary-teacher, W. D. Alexander in 1864, just a scant 40 years after the first printing presses were set up in the Sandwich Islands.

Bolstered by the granting of statehood to Hawaii in 1959, interest in the unique background of the newest state has increased the need for textbooks such as Alexander's early work. There is much to be gained—philologically and otherwise—from the reprinting of this classic study by a devoted educator.

PREFACE.

As all former grammars of the Hawaiian language are out of print, at the solicitation of friends, I have revised and enlarged a brief synopsis of Hawaiian grammar, which was originally written for my pupils, and published in 1864.

This little work does not pretend to be a philosophical treatise, or to be a complete account of the structure and peculiarities of the Hawaiian branch of the Polynesian language. But it is hoped that it may be of service to those who wish to study the genuine, uncorrupted idiom as spoken by the older Hawaiians, as well as to students of comparative philology.

The terms and divisions of European grammars have been retained for the convenience of students, although they are only partially applicable to languages of a radically different type.

I have to acknowledge my obligations to Rev. L. Andrews' Hawaiian Grammar, to Dr. Maunsell's New Zealand Grammar, and to M. Gaussin's able work on the Polynesian language.

W. D. ALEXANDER.

CONTENTS.

PART I.

PART II.

A Short Synopsis of Hawaiian Grammar.

PART I.

The following synopsis is intended to contain only general principles.

ORTHOEPY.

§ 1. All purely Hawaiian sounds can be represented by twelve letters, of which five are vowels and seven consonants, viz: a, e, i, o, u, h, k, l, m, n, p, w. *A* is sounded as in f*a*ther, *e* as in th*ey*, *i* as in mar*i*ne, *o* as in n*o*te, *u* as in r*u*le, and not as in m*u*le. In a few words, as *maka, make, mana,* &c., the sound of *a* approaches that of a short *u* in t*u*b. In the compounds of *waho* and in *Oahu,* it has a broad sound like that of a in f*a*ll.

§ 2. No distinction was formerly made between the sounds of *k* and *t* or between those of *l* and *r*. The sound of *t* prevailed on Kauai, that of *k* on Hawaii. In the words "Hilo," "lilo" and "hilahila," the *l* was often sounded like *d*. It is on some accounts unfortunate that *k* was chosen rather than *t* to represent the sound which is represented by *t* throughout the rest of Polynesia, while the Polynesian "k" corresponds to the guttural of the Hawaiian dialect. The sound of *w* is really between that of *v* and *w*, in English, and in the middle of words it approaches more closely to that of *v*, as in *hewa, lawa,* &c.

§ 3. Every word and syllable must end in a vowel, and no two consonants are ever heard without a vowel sound between them. To this rule there is no exception.

§ 4. Besides the sounds mentioned above, there is in many words a guttural break or catching of the breath, sometimes at the beginning, but more often in the middle of a word. This guttural is properly a consonant, and forms an *essential* part of the words in which it is found. It almost invariably

takes the place of the Polynesian *k.* Thus the Polynesian *ika,*
fish, becomes *i'a* in Hawaiian. This guttural consonant is
represented by an apostrophe, in a few common words, to
distinguish their meaning, as *ko'u,* my, *kou,* thy.

§ 5. A list of a few of the more important words distinguished by the guttural break:

ae, to assent.
ai, food.
ao, light, a cloud.
au, a current, time, &c.
āu, thine.
akoakoa, to assemble.
ea, rise up.
ia, he, she or it.
ie, climbing plant.

ī, mouldy
oá, to split.
ōī, to excel.
ōō, a digger.
ou, thine.
ui, question.
hai, to tell.
hao, iron.
hiu, shy.
hua, fruit.
huaka'i, procession.
hui, to mix, unite.
kai, seawater.
koa, a soldier, brave.
koe, remaining.
koi, to urge, compel.
kou, thine.
kui, to stitch, a needle.
liuliu, to get ready.
mai, hither.
makau, fish-hook.
moa, a chicken, fowl.
nău, to chew.
nāu, for thee.
pau, done, finished.
poi, taro paste.
pue, to crouch.
wau, I.

a'e, to pass over, embark.
a-i, neck, Polynesian *kaki.*
a'o, to teach.
a'u, a sword-fish.
a'u, mine.
ako'ako'a, the horned coral.
ē'a, a cloud of dust.
i'a, a fish.
i'e, a kapa beater.
i'e, quarrelsome in liquor.
i'i, to be crowded.
ó'a, a rafter.
ó'i, to limp.
ó'o, ripe.
o'u, mine.
u'i, young, vigorous.
ha'i, to be broken.
ha'o, to discredit.
hi'u, a fish's tail.
hu'a, foam.
hu'akai, sea foam, sponge.
hu'i, rheumatism.
ka'i, to carry, lead.
ko'a, coral reef.
ko'e, an angle worm.
ko'i, an axe.
ko'u, mine.
ku'i, to pound.
li'uli'u, a long time.
ma'i, sick.
maka'u, afraid.
mo'a, cooked, well done.
na'u, for me.

pa'u, soot.
po'i, a cover, lid.
pu'e, to seduce, to hill potatoes.
wa'u, to scratch.

§ 6. It is important to observe the distinction between long and short vowels. Thus *ăwa* means a harbor, but *āwa*, a plant from which an intoxicating drink is made. Again, *kăua* means war, while *kāua* means we two, or I and thou. *Măui* is the name of an island, *Māui* of a famous demigod, and *kăula* means a rope, while *kāula* means a prophet.

§ 7. The accent generally falls on the penult. This is true of about five-sixths of the words in the language.

§ 8. The accent is frequently drawn forward by the enclitic *la,* which is generally pronounced as if it formed part of the preceding word. Thus, *aku* la is pronounced *akúla, ua moku la* as *ua mokúla.*

§ 9. A List of Similar words distinguished by the Accent.

áia, there.	aiá, ungodly, impious.
áka, shadow.	aká, but.
ála, to rise.	alá, a pebble.
áno, likeness, character.	anó, now, immediately.
éha, pain.	ehá, four.
í'o, meat.	i-ó, yonder.
ína, if.	iná, come on ! be quick !
ó'o, ripe.	oó, a digger.
óo, a bird.	
úe, to wrench, turn.	ué, to cry.
káka, to rinse clothes.	kaká, to split wood.
kála, to proclaim, to pardon.	kālá, a dollar, silver.
kéla, to excel.	kelá, that.
kéna, to be satiated, of thirst.	kená, to order, send on duty.
kanáka, man.	kánaka, men, people.
málu, a shadow.	malú, secret.
máma, to chew.	māmá, active, light.
maláma, month.	málama, to take care.
nána, for him.	naná, to look, to see.
póho, chalk.	pohó, to sink.
púa, a flower.	puá, a bundle, a flock.
wáhi, a place.	wahí, to wrap up.

ETYMOLOGY.

§ 10. The Hawaiian language has no inflections whatever. All grammatical relations such as number, case, tense, &c., are expressed by separate particles.

§ 11. Most words in this language can be used either as nouns, adjectives, verbs or adverbs, their meaning being indicated by their position in the sentence, and by the accompanying particles.

NOUNS.

§ 12. The Gender of nouns is distinguished, first, by the use of entirely different words, as *elemakule,* old man, and *luahine,* old woman. Second, by the use of the adjectives *kane,* male, and *wahine,* female, as *moa kane,* a cock, and *moa wahine,* a hen.

§ 13. The Plural Number is distinguished,

First, by the use of the plural definite article *na* before the noun, as *na hale,* the houses.

Second, by the use of the *plural sign mau,* which is used chiefly of small numbers from two to ten inclusive. It does not admit the definite article *ka* or *ke* before it, but is generally preceded by the indefinite article *he,* or by a possessive or demonstrative pronoun, as *keia mau mea,* these things; *ku'u mau maka,* my eyes; *he mau lio,* several horses.

Third, by the use of the plural signs, *poe, pae,* and *pu'u,* which are properly collective nouns, and take the articles or other qualifying words before them. *Poe* is used chiefly of living beings, and means a company, collection. *Pu'u,* literally a heap, is used chiefly of lifeless things, and *pae* of lands, islands, &c. E. g., *he poe haumana,* a company of disciples; *he pu'u pohaku,* a pile of stones; *keia pae moku,* these islands.

Fourth. A few words, besides the methods explained above, also distinguish the plural by prolonging and accenting the first syllable. Thus *kănáka,* man, plural *kānaka, wăhine,* woman, plural *wāhine,* and a few others.

Fifth. The syllable *ma* appended to the name of a person, denotes the company associated with him, as *Hoapili ma,* Hoapili and his company.

PREPOSITIONS.

§ 14. The distinctions of case are expressed by means of prepositions. The simple prepositions are as follows:

1. { A and O
     Ka and Ko } equivalent to "of."

   E. g., "Ka piko o ka mauna," the summit of the mountain; "Ko ke alii aina," the chief's land; "ka hana a ke kauwa," the work of the servant; "wahi a ke alii," the chief said so.

2. Na and No, *of, for, concerning, on account of.* "No" also sometimes *from,* in which case the following noun takes the directive *mai* after it. E. g., "No na alii ka aina," the land belongs to the chiefs; "na mea a'u i lohe ai no Lono," the things which I heard concerning Lono; "no Amerika mai ka moku," the ship is from America; "no ia mau mea," concerning those matters.

3. I, Ia and Io, *to, at* of time, and *by* with adjectives and neuter verbs. *I* is also used before what in other grammars is called a predicate accusative, after verbs signifying to change, to choose, render or constitute, to become, or to be changed into.

   I is also the sign of the objective case after transitive verbs. In certain common phrases a verb is understood before the objective sign, as "i wai," bring water; "i pahi," get me a knife," &c. E. g., "E hai aku i keia poe kanaka," tell to these men. "e hele i ke kuahiwi," go to the mountain; "i ka po," in the night; "piha i ka wai," full of water; "ma'i i ke anu," ill from cold; "e kukulu i ka hale," to build the house; "ua lilo ia i kahuna," he became a priest; "ua hanaia i makau," it was made into a hook, "ua koho au ia Keawe *i* elele," I have chosen Keawe as messenger.

4. Ma, *at* or *in*, of place, and *by* before pronouns and names of persons, in which case it takes *o* after it, and the enclitic *la* or *nei* after the following noun or pronoun.

   E. g., "Ua noho oia ma Waimea," he lived at Waimea; "ma o Iesú la," by Jesus.

5. Mai, *from.* The following noun takes *mai* or *aku* after it, according as the direction is towards or away from the speaker.

   Mai takes *o* after it before pronouns, and *a* before names of persons in relation to time, sometimes written *ia.*

   E. g., "Mai ka waha mai," from the mouth; "mai Honolulu aku i Kailua," from Honolulu to Kailua; "mai o'u aku nei," from me; "mai ka po mai," since the night; "mai a Wakea," from the time of Wakea.

   Me, *with.* E. g., "E hele pu me ia," go together with him. As an adverb, *me* means "as," "like." E. g., "Me he hipa la," like a sheep; "e like me keia," like this; "me ka ai ole," without food.

   E, *by,* only used after passive verbs, to denote the agent. E. g., "Ua kukuluia ka hale e ke alii," the house has been built by the chief.

REMARKS ON THE PREPOSITIONS.

The Distinction between A and O.

§ 15. There is an important distinction between the three *a* prepositions, *a, ka,* and *na,* and the three *o* prepositions, *o ko,* and *no.* "*O*" implies a *passive* or *intransitive* relation. "*a*" an *active* and *transitive* one. "A" can only be used before a word denoting a living person or agent, and implies that the thing possessed is his to make or act upon, or is subject to his will, while "o" implies that it is his merely to possess or use, to receive or be affected by. This distinction is common to all Polynesian languages, but is most clear and striking in that of New Zealand. Thus "ka hale a Keawe" means "the house which Keawe built," but "ka hale o Keawe" means simply "the house which Keawe lives in." Again, "ka wahine a Keawe" means "the wife of Keawe," while "ka wahine o Keawe" would mean Keawe's maid-servant. "Ke keiki a Keawe" denotes Keawe's own child, while "ke keiki o Keawe" would denote his errand boy, &c. In New Zealand, "he hangi *mau*" is an oven for you to cook with, but "he hangi *mou*" is an oven in which you are to be cooked, and would be a most offensive curse.

§ 16. It follows of course that such words as *"hana,"* work, require *a* after them, and so does *ai,* food, and all its derivatives. *Words* are conceived as of made, or fashioned by the mouth, and hence *"olelo," "pule,"* &c., require *a.* For a similar reason *"palapala,"* writing, takes *a.* The following names of relationship, *keiki,* child, *mo'opuna,* a descendant, *kauwá,* a servant, and *haumana,* a pupil, require *a* after them. On the other hand, our parents, brothers and sisters, our ancestors, rulers, and friends, take *o,* since they do not owe their existence to us, nor are subject to our will. O is used of clothing, canoes, and such things as are ours to wear or use, but not to produce. All the parts of the body, and the faculties of the mind, as *mana'o, makemake,* &c., take o. All the more remote relations, including that of a part to a whole, are expressed by *o.*

§ 17. The following list comprises the principal words that generally require the *a* prepositions after them.

ai, food.	kauoha, command.	palapala, writing.
oihana, office.	kauwá, servant.	pule, prayer.
olelo, word.	kane, husband.	wanana, prophecy.
haumana, disciple.	keiki, child.	wahine, wife.
hana, work.	mo'opuna, descendant.	buke, book.

On Ka and Ko.

§ 18. The prepositions *ka* and *ko* are called *prefix prepositions,* because when they are used, the noun denoting the possessor *precedes* the thing possessed. Thus, "ko ke alii hale," the chief's house, is equivalent to "ka hale o ke alii," the house of the chief. These prefix prepositions are undoubtedly compounded of the definite article *ka* and the prepositions *a* and *o* respectively. Thus, "ko ke alii hale" is for "ka-o ke alii hale."

On Na and No.

§ 19. The fundamental idea in *na* and *no* seems to be *right* or *possession*. Thus, "no ke alii ka hale" means the house is for or belongs to the chief. When an *active* verb in the infinitive follows *na* is used and not *no*. As, "na Keawe e a'o aku i na kanaka," it belongs to Keawe, it is K.'s *duty* to teach men. *"No* Hilo mai," from Hilo, implies that one *belongs* to Hilo. No denotes *origin* from, mai *separation* from. Both *no* and *mai* signifying *from*, require a directive, *mai* or *aku*, after the following noun, according as the motion is towards or away from the speaker.

On I, Ia and Io.

§ 20. The preposition *i*, to, and *i*, the objective sign, are really distinct words. In the New Zealand, Tongan and Rarotongan dialects, the former is *ki*, and the latter *i*. They take the form *ia* before pronouns and proper names. The form *io*, to, is used after verbs of motion, before pronouns or proper names, which are generally followed by *nei* or *la*. E. g., "io makou nei," to us, "io Kristó la," to Christ. The *a* in *ia*, and the *o* in *io* are no doubt distinct elements, and in some dialects are written separately. Probably like the "O emphatic," they express personality or individuality.

The use of *i* as a sign of the objective case may be illustrated by the use of the preposition *á* in Spanish before the direct object of a verb, when it denotes an animated being. In a similar manner *eth* is used in Hebrew before a definite object.

E. g., "Puhi lakou *i* ka hale," they burned the house.

§ 21. What is called the vocative case, is expressed by the prefix *e*, as "E Keoni!" O John!

ARTICLES.

§ 22. *"He"* is the Hawaiian *indefinite article*, corresponding to the English *a* or *an*. It is used only in the singular number and *nominative* case. After a verb or preposition the article "a," is often rendered by "kahi" or "kekahi." Its use before the plural signs *mau*, *poe*, &c., can be explained by the fact that these are properly collective nouns.

§ 23. There are two definite articles, corresponding to the English *"the,"* *ka* or *ke* for the singular, and *na* for the plural. The form *ke* is used before *all* words beginning with *k*, a few beginning with *p*, and a large number beginning with *a* or *o*. The form *te* prevails throughout all Southern Polynesia. This article, *ke*, must not be confounded with the particle *ke* prefixed to verbs.

§ 24. The best rule for the form of the definite article before words commencing with *a* is the following. Use *ke* before ă short, and *ka* before ā long. Thus *ke* ăwa, the harbor, and *ka* āwa, the plant *awa*. L. Gaussin says that *ka* is used before those words at the beginning of which a consonant (the Polynesian *k* guttural) has been dropped, and *ke* before the simple vowels *a* and *o*. These two rules generally coincide.

§ 25. The following are the most common words commencing with *a, o* and *p* that require the article *ke* before them.

ke a, the jaw	ke aloha, love	ke o'a, rafter
ke a'a, root, vein	ke ama, outrigger	ke oho, hair
ke ao, light	ke ami, hinge	ke ola, life
ke aupuni, kingdom	ke aniani, glass	ke ola'i, earthquake
ke ahi, fire	ke ana, cave	ke olo, saw
ke ahiahi, evening	ke anaina, assembly	ke one, sand
ke aho, breath	ke ano, likeness	ke ope, bundle
ke aka, shadow	ke anu, cold	ke mele, song
ke akaakai, rushes	ke apo, ring, hoop	ke pa, plate
ke akua, God	ke awa, harbor	ke pio, prisoner
ke ala, road	ke awakea, noon	ke pihi, button
ke ali'i, the chief	ke ea, breath	ke po'i, cover
ke alo, front	ke o, fork	ke po'o, head

The 'O Emphatic.

§ 26. The "'O emphatic," as it is generally called, *ko* in New Zealand, seems to be a kind of article. It serves to point out the subject emphatically. It is used only with the nominative case, and chiefly before proper names and pronouns. It is the regular prefix to a proper name in the nominative case.

§ 27. It occurs with *common nouns* only when they are *defined* or particularized by the definite article, by an adjective pronoun or a noun in the possessive case, and when at the same time they begin the clause. It may be added that it occurs with such nouns only when in English they would be the subject of the verb "to be," in a clause affirming the identity of two terms, or when they stand in the nominative absolute.

Examples of 'O Emphatic.

"Holo aku la o Lono," Lono sailed away. "O oe no ke kanaka," thou art the man. "O ko'u lio keia," this is my horse. "O Hawaii ka mokupuni nui," Hawaii is the large island.

ADJECTIVES.

§ 28. Adjectives have no distinction of Gender, Number or Case.

They are compared by subjoining adverbs to them. The adverbs *a'e*, and *aku* are used to form the comparative degree, and *loa*, "very," to form the superlative. The preposition *i* is sometimes used like "than" in English, and then means "in comparison with." Comparison is also often expressed by using the verb *oi*, to surpass. E. g., "Na mea nui aku i keia," things greater than this. "Oi aku keia mamua o kela," this surpasses, goes *before* that. "E oi aku ko oukou maikai i ko lakou," your beauty will surpass theirs.

NUMERALS.

§ 29. The Cardinal numbers are as follows:

1	kahi	11	umikumamakahi
2	lua	12	umikumamalua
3	kolu	20	iwakalua
4	ha	21	iwakaluakumamakahi
5	lima	30	kanakolu
6	ono	40	kanaha
7	hiku	400	lau
8	walu	4,000	mano
9	iwa	40,000	kini
10	umi	400,000	lehu

[The following have been introduced by the American missionaries] :

50	kanalima	90	kanaiwa
60	kanaono	100	haneri
70	kanahiku	1,000	tausani
80	kanawalu	1,000,000	miliona, &c.

Formerly 100 would have been expressed thus, "elua kanaha me ka iwakalua."

REMARKS.

§ 30. Instead of counting by pairs as in most of the southern groups, the Hawaiians counted by fours. A four taken collectively is called a *kauna* and formed the basis of their system. This probably arose from the custom of counting fish, coconuts, taro, &c., by taking a couple in each hand, or by tying them in bundles of four.

The word *kumi* or *'umi* is used in the other dialects only in counting fathoms. On the other hand *anahulu,* which is used in Hawaiian only for a period of ten days, is the word for ten in all the other Malayo-Polynesian languages. Besides, they have for forty the specific numerals, *iako,* used in counting tapas, and canoes, and *ka'au,* used in counting fish, the Southern *tekau.*

§ 31. In counting *a* is generally prefixed to the numerals, as *akahi, alua,* &c. At other times *e* is generally prefixed. But the Hawaiian dialect generally uses *ho'o* before *kahi,* as *ho'okahi pua'a,* one hog, &c. As Gaussin says, *a* contains the idea of succession, and of change, *e,* of completion, or of permanent state. The higher numbers are used like collective nouns, and like them take the articles before them, as *he umi, he kanaha,* &c. Compare the expressions *a* hundred, *a* score, &c., in English. The units are connected to the tens by the connective *kumama,* as has been seen above. But the higher numbers are connected by *me* followed by the article, as "ho'okahi haneri me ka iwakaluakumamahiku," = 127.

ORDINAL AND DISTRIBUTIVE NUMBERS.

§ 32. The ordinals are formed by prefixing the article *ka* or *ke* to the cardinal numbers, except "the first," which is "*mua.*" "The third day" is "ke kolu o ka la," "The seventh year," "ka hiku o ka makahiki." Distributives are formed by prefixing *pa,* as *pakahi,* one by one, or one apiece, *palua,* two by two, or two apiece, &c. Sometimes *koko'o* is prefixed, to denote company, or partnership, as *koko'olima,* five in company, *koko'olua,* a second, a partner or assistant.

FRACTIONS.

§ 33. No Polynesian language had originally any word to express the idea of definite fraction, though they had an abundance of words to express the idea of a part. To supply this defect, the English Missionaries introduced into Tahitian the words *afa* (half) and *tuata* (quarter). In a similar way the word *hapa* (half) has been introduced into the Hawaiian language, but has acquired the general signification of a part. By prefixing this *hapa* to the several numerals, names have been formed for all possible fractions, as "hapalua," a half, "hapaha," a fourth, &c.

PRONOUNS.

§ 34. The personal pronouns are as follows:

	1ST PERSON	2D PERSON	3D PERSON
Singular	Au or Owau	Oe	Ia or Oia
Dual	Māua, Kāua	Oukou	Lāua
Plural	Makou, Kakou	Olua	Lakou

REMARKS.

§ 35. *Owau* is simply a more emphatic form for *au,* as *oia* is for *ia.* The dual was formed by compounding the root of the pronoun with *"lua,"* two, and the plural in like manner by adding *"kolu,"* three, to the root. Hence these plurals were originally *trinals,* as they are still in Vitian or Feejee, which has four numbers. The *l's* have been dropped in all cases except in *"olua,"* but are still retained in the plural by the Tongan dialect, as *mautolu,* &c. None of the pronouns have any distinction of gender.

§ 36. The forms *maua* and *makou exclude* while *kaua* and *kakou include* the person spoken to. This remarkable distinction is found in all Polynesian languages, as well as in those of Micronesia, and even extends to the East Indian Archipelago. In the second person the Hawaiian has dropped initial *k,* using *oe* for *koe,* &c.

§ 37. In the singular number the Personal pronouns have a second, shorter set of forms, or pronominal affixes, used only after certain prepositions, (a, o, ka, ko, na, no, ia, and io), with which they unite to form part of the same word. These forms are in the first person *'u,* in the second, *u,* in the third, *na.* This *'u* in the first person is *ku* in the S. W. dialects of Polynesia.

§ 38. The Declension of these pronouns in the singular is as follows :

		1ST PERSON.	2D PERSON.	3D PERSON.		
Nominative		Au	Oe	Ia		
With the Preposition					*Less Common.*	
Of	A	a'u	au	ana	a ia	
	O	o'u	ou	ona	o ia	la nei
	Ka	ka'u	kau	kana	ka ia	la nei
	Ko	ko'u	kou	kona	ko ia	la nei
For &c.	Na	na'u	nau	nana		
	No	no'u	nou	nona	no ia	la nei
To	Ia	ia'u	ia oe	ia ia		
	Io	io'u	la nei	i ou	la nei	i ona la
By or Through—Ma	ma o'u	la nei	ma ou	la nei	ma ona la	
From—Mai	mai o'u	aku mai	mai ou	aku mai	mai ona	aku mai
With—Me	me a'u		me oe		me ia	
By—E	e au		e oe		e ia	

The form iá ia, him, is pronounced as one word, with the accent on the first syllable, like yáya.

§ 39. The duals of the personal pronouns often serve to connect words denoting persons. Thus, "Hoapili *laua* o Kalanimoku." The dual *laua* includes them both. In such sentences, *"O"* follows the dual when both nouns are subjects of the same verb, as *laua o* in the preceding example. "E olelo pu maua me Manono" means, I will talk with Manono, *"maua"* by an apparent confusion of ideas, including the speaker and Manono.

§ 40. The Hawaiians generally avoid applying *laua* or *lakou* to inanimate objects. The same remark applies to *ia ia*. They use *"ia mea"* or some such phrase instead of a personal pronoun.

§ 41. *"Self"* and *"own"* are expressed by *iho* placed after the pronoun. *Himself* is ia ia iho," and *his own* "kona iho."

Examples of Pronouns.

"Ka hana a'u," my work. "Aole o'u lio," I have no horse. "Heaha kou manao no'u," what is your opinion of me. "Ua hoopunipuni mai olua ia'u," you two have lied to me. "Ma o'u la ua maluhia keia aina," through me this land was in peace. "Ua pepehi ia oia e au," he was killed by me. "He hale ko kaua," you and I have a house. "Ua malama mai oe ia maua," you have taken care of us two. "Aloha oe a me na hanai au," love to thee and thy foster children. "He manao ko'u ia oe." I have a thought to you. "Ma ou la e lanakila ai makou," through you we shall conquer. "Ua lawe ia ia mea mai ou aku la," that thing was taken away from you. "Malaila no ia," there he is. "E kokua oe ia ia," help thou him. "Hele mai la lakou io na la," they came to him. "Mai hoohiki ma ona la," do not swear by him. "Haliu aku ia mai ona aku," he turned away from him. "Uwe pu laua," they two wept together. "Ao aku la ia ia lakou," he taught them. "Ma o lakou la e hoouna ai oe," by them do thou send. "Mai o lakou aku ka leo kaua," from them was the voice of war.

POSSESSIVE PRONOUNS.

§ 42. The Possessive pronouns are simply the personal pronouns preceded by the prepositions, *a, o, ka,* and *ko,* i.e., the first four forms in section 38. Besides these we find the possessive, *ku'u,* my, which is used for both *ka'u* and *ko'u;* and *ko,* a contraction of *kou,* thy, which is used for either *kau* or *kou* with certain common words. *Ku'u* and *ko* seem more familiar, and less formal than the regular forms. The distinction between the *a* and the *o* forms must be observed.

Examples of Possessives.

"Kau mau keiki," thy children. "Ko makou hale," our house. "Ka oukou hana," your work. "Kana kauoha," his command. "Kona makua," his parent. "Ka'u palapala," my writing. "Kuu hoa," my comrade. "Ko'u lio," my horse.

DEMONSTRATIVE PRONOUNS.

§ 43. The Demonstrative pronouns are as follows:

Ia, *that,* the most general of the demonstratives. It never admits the preposition *i* before it, i.e., *"i ia"* is contracted into *"ia."*

Keia, *this* ⎫ These two are used in contrast or opposition.
Kelá, *that* ⎬ Kela generally precedes keia, as in the phrase
　　　　　 ⎭ "kela me keia," this and that, "kela mea keia mea," everything.

Neia, *this, the present.* It is often used of time, as "i neia la," today.

Ua-nei, ⎫ With these demonstratives the noun is inserted be-
Ua-la, ⎭ tween the two parts of the pronoun, as "ua móku la," that ship. Compare the French, *"ce* livre *ci,"* this book (here). They generally refer back to something just mentioned. They are also used with proper names, in which case the *o* emphatic is often expressed after *ua,* as "ka olelo ana a *ua* o Maui *nei."*

Examples of Demonstrative Pronouns.

E. g., "Ka wahahee o ia olelo," the falsehood of that speech. "E haalele ia hana," leave that work. "Heaha kela mea nui?" what is that great thing? "Ma keia pae aina," at these islands. "O Keawe ka inoa o ua kanaká la," Keawe is that man's name.

INTERROGATIVE PRONOUNS.

§ 44. The Interrogative Pronouns are as follows:

Wai, *who? which?* In the nominative case, Owai, it is used of individual things as well as persons, but after prepositions, only of persons. It is never used adjectively, i. e. to qualify a noun.

Aha, *what?* It takes *"he"* before it in the nominative, as "heaha?" but *ke* after prepositions, as "no keaha?" for what. It always refers to inanimate things, not persons, and is never used adjectively with a noun.

Hea, *which?* It is strictly an interrogative adjective, and always follows its noun, as "he kumu hea ia," what sort of a teacher is he? The compounds of *"hea"* serve as interrogative adverbs.

Examples of Interrogative Pronouns.

"Owai kona inoa?" what is his name? "Nowai ka lio?" whose is the horse? "Me wai oe i hele ai?" with whom did you go? "Heaha kau i hana 'i?" what hast thou done? "Ma ka hale hea?" in which house?

INDEFINITE PRONOUNS.

§ 45. Among Indefinite Pronouns may be reckoned:

Hai, *another,* which is used only after prepositions, and never occurs in the nominative case. E.g., "ko hai waiwai," another's property. "Haawi oia ia hai," he gave to another.

Wahi, *some, a little.* It was originally a noun, but is now used adjectively, as "wahi ai," some food, "wahi laau," some timber, "ua wahi kanaka nei," this fellow, "kela wahi kanaka," that fellow. Here it has a depreciatory or diminutive force. It never takes the article *ka* before it, but very often is preceded by *he,* and rarely by *na.*

Kauwahi, *some part, some.* It is a compound of the preceding, and is always used in a partitive sense. It is sometimes preceded by the definite article *ke,* as "ke kau-wahi o ka olelo a ke Akua," a little of the word of God.

Kahi, *one, a, a certain.* It is the same as the numeral one, but has acquired a degree of indefiniteness, like the English *a* or *an,* which originally was the same as the numeral *one.* E.g., "Eia kahi hewa hou," here is a new sin. "Eia na inoa o kahi mau mea," here are the names of certain persons.

Kekahi, *a certain, some.* The article *ke,* prefixed to *kahi* gives it greater individuality. E.g., "i kekahi wa," upon a certain time. When repeated it means "some—others." Thus, "ua nui no kekahi bele, a ua uuku loa ho'i kekahi," i. e. some bells are large and others quite small. The phrase "kekahi i kekahi" is used in a reciprocal sense, and means "each other," "one another." E. g., "E aloha aku oukou i kekahi i kekahi," love one another. *Kekahi* placed after the subject of a sentence means "also," "also another," as "owau kekahi," I also. "O oukou anei *kekahi* i makemake e hele aku?" do you *too* wish to go away?

E, *other, different.* This is properly an adjective, but it may be well to mention it in this connection. Its original Polynesian form seems to have been *kese,* of which we find the variations *kehe, ese, ké* and *é.* By itself, it means "strange," "foreign," but when followed by the directives *a'e* or *aku,* it means *"other."* E. g., "he mea é," a strange thing. "Na mea *e a'e,*" the other things. "All" is expressed by "*a pau*" following the noun or pronoun which it modifies.

VERBS.

§ 46. All the distinctions of tense, mode and voice are expressed by separate particles, while number and person are regarded as accidents of the subject and not of the verb. The tenses are not nearly as definite as in English. In fact the distinctions of *time,* which in other languages are considered of so much importance, are but little regarded in Hawaiian, while the chief attention is paid to the accidents of *place.* The following is

A Synopsis of the Verb Hana in the Active Voice.

Present,	ke hana nei au	I work.
Past 1st form,	hana au	I worked.
" 2nd form,	i hana au	I worked.
Perfect,	ua hana au	I have worked.
Pluperfect,	ua hana e au	I had worked.
Future,	e hana au	I shall work.
Imperative,	e hana oe	work thou.
Infinitive,	e hana	to work.
Present or } Participle, Imperfect }	e hana ana	working.
Past Participle,	i hana	{ having worked or { who had worked.

§ 47. The following is the order in which the verb and its adjuncts are placed:

1st. The tense signs, as *i, ua, e,* &c.
2d. The verb itself.
3d. The qualifying adverb, as *mau, wale, ole, pu,* &c.
4th. The passive sign, *ia.*
5th. The verbal directives, as *aku, mai,* &c.
6th. The locatives, *nei* or *la,* or the particles *ana* or *ai.*
7th. The strengthening particle, *no.*
8th. The subject.
9th. The object or predicate noun.

Of course the above mentioned elements are never all found together at once. Of the particles in the sixth place, *nei la, ana* and *ai,* if one is used, the others are excluded, except in a few cases where *la* is used after *ana.* E. g., "E hana mua ia aku ana no ke alanui."

REMARKS ON THE TENSES.

§ 48. The verb without any prefix has generally a past meaning. This is the regular form for the leading verb in past time, especially at the beginning of a sentence. In this case it is generally followed by *la*, e.g., "i mai la," he said; "hoi mai la lakou," they returned; "noho no oia ma Oahu," he lived at Oahu; "alaila, kuka ihó la lakou," then they took counsel; "ke hai aku nei au ia oe," I inform you; "ke noi aku nei makou ia ia," we entreat him; "aole au e hana hou pela," I will not do so again.

I.

The prefix *i* is used in negative sentences after *aole*, and in all relative sentences in past time. It never begins an unqualified sentence. When it begins a statement, a qualifying clause follows, expressing a reason, purpose, time, &c. E. g., "I hele mai nei au e hai aku ia oe," I have come here to inform you; "aole oia *i* ae mai," he did not consent; "i ka wa *i noho* ai o Kamehameha," at the time when Kamehameha lived.

Ua.

The prefix *ua* is never used in a negative clause beginning with *aole*, nor in what would be a relative clause in English. It has been questioned whether it is properly a tense sign. We think that it affirms the completion of an action or the resulting state, and hence corresponds most nearly to the English perfect with "have." It also differs from *i* in this, that it affirms absolutely, and without limitation, while *i* is limited or qualified in construction. The adverbs *mai nei*, "just now," after a verb preceded by *ua*, express most truly the distinction of the perfect tense in English.

The adverb *e* after the verb means "before," and so helps to form a sort of pluperfect. But "e hana e au" does not mean "I shall have worked," but "I shall previously work."

E. g., "Ua hele mai na kanaka," the men have come; "ua ike au i kou ano," I have known your character; "ua hina iho nei ka hale," the house has just fallen; "ua lilo *e* ke aupuni ia ia," the kingdom had been transferred to him.

IMPERATIVE PARTICLES.

Instead of *"e,"* the regular prefix of the imperative, "o" or "ou" is sometimes used, as a mild command. The particle "ua" seems to be used as an imperative sign before "oki," to cut off, as "ua oki pela," stop there. A prohibition is expressed by placing "mai" before the verb.

E. g., "Ou hoi oukou," return ye; "o hele oe," go thou. "Ua oki oe i ka olelo," stop your talk. "Mai hana hou oe pela," don't do so again. This must not be confounded with the adverb, "mai," which means nearly, almost. E. g., "Mai

make au," I was near dying; "mai haule ia," he came near
falling.

On the Particles Ana and No.

§ 49. The affix *ana,* which corresponds to the ending "ing."
in Englsih, denotes *continuance,* and may be present, past or
future. Thus "e hana ana au," may mean "I am working."
or "I was working," or "I will be working," according to the
connection. *Ana* is affixed to the passive as well as to the
active. Like "ing" in English, *ana* often forms a participial
noun. But in this case *ana* always *precedes* the directives
aku or *mai.* Compare "E holo *mai ana,*" he is sailing hither,
and "kona holo *ana mai,*" his sailing hither. It may be separated from the verb by an adverb.

The infinitive after *hiki,* and sometimes after *pono,* takes
ke before it, instead of *e.*

The particle *no* is intensive, and serves to emphasize an
assertion. It is often found also with adjectives and nouns,
where it helps to express the idea of the verb "to be."

E. g., "I ko'u hele ana 'ku," in my going, i.e., while I am
going. "E kukulu hale ana ia," he is house building. "E
mahi ia ana ka ai," the food is being cultivated. "Oia ke
kolu o kona holo ana mai," that was the third (time) of his
sailing hither. Aole ona manao e hele," he had no intention
to go. "He pono ia oe ke kokua mai," it is right for you to
help.

The Passive Voice.

§ 50. The Passive sign is *ia* affixed to the verb. The
tenses of the passive voice are formed in the same way as
those of the active. As, "hanaia iho la na mea a pau e ia,"
all things were made by him. Sometimes another letter is
inserted between the verb and *ia,* as *kaulia,* the passive of
kau, and *auhulihia,* from *auhuli, loohia,* &c. A few words
omit the *i,* as *ikea,* passive of *ike,* to know, and *lohea,* the
passive of *lohe,* to hear.

In the New Zealand dialect the common mode of expressing the *imperative* of a transitive verb is by its *passive.*
Traces of this occur in Hawaiian. E. g., *imiia* ka oukou
pono," seek your own advantage, *Laieikawai,* p. 62. *"Kaheaia*
ko kupuna-wahine," call your grandmother, id. p. 64. So
oleloia, nohoia, in the same work.

The Causative Form.

§ 51. By prefixing *ho'o,* sometimes *ho,* before a vowel, and
sometimes *ha'a* to the verb, a causative verb is formed.
(This *ha'a* is the older form, as we see from the forms
whaka, faka, fa'a and *ha'a* of the other dialects.)   Thus

from *a,* to burn, we get *hoā,* to kindle, and from *komo,* to
enter, *ho'okomo,* to cause to   enter, &c. Any verb in the
language may take this prefix. From *like* is formed *hooha-
like,* to cause to be like, and from *inu,* to drink, *hoohainu,*
to cause to drink, to give drink to.

Verbal Directives, &c.

§ 52. That which is denoted by a verb in Hawaiian, is
generally conceived of as having a motion or tendency in
some direction, which is expressed by one of the following
particles :

Mai, hither, this way, towards the speaker.

Aku, away, onwards, from the speaker.

A'e, upwards, or sideways.

Iho, down.

In narration, *iho* means "thereupon," "immediately after,"
and generally "as a consequence." *Aku* and *ae* are also used
of time, as "kela la aku," and "ia la ae," the next day, "ma
keia hope aku," hereafter, &c.

The particles *nei* or *la* were originally used to indicate
locality, like "here" and "there," and are opposed to each
other in meaning. *Nei* means present in place and time,
here and now, while *la* denotes distance in place, but not
necessarily in time. *La* unites with the "directives" so as
to form one word with them in pronunciation, and after
aku, iho and *a'e,* it shifts the accent to the last syllable, as
ihóla, akúla, a'éla.

The Relative Particle Ai.

§ 53. *Ai* is a relative particle, and often supplies the want
of a relative pronoun. It follows the verb, and refers back
to a preceding noun, or to an adverb or adverbial phrase
expressing time, place, cause or manner. The initial *a,* is
often dropped after a verb ending with *a,* and after the
passive sign ia, as *hana'i, loaa'i, hunaia'i,* &c. It is sometimes omitted when *nei, ana* or *la* takes its place. It must
be used :

First, in relative clauses in which the relative would be the
object of the verb in English, as "the things *which* he saw,"
na mea ana i ike *ai.*

Second, in relative clauses in which the relative refers to
a *thing,* which is the means, cause or instrument *by which*
any thing is or is done, as "Eia ka *mea* i make *ai* na kanaka," here is the cause from *which* the people died.

Third, in relative clauses, where in English the relative
adverbs *when* or *where* would be used, referring to a *time*

or *place* in which any thing is or is done, as "I ka la a makou i hiki mai *ai,*" on the day *when* we arrived.

Fourth, when an adverb or adverbial phrase expressing time, place, cause or manner, stands for emphasis at the beginning of the sentence. E. g., *"Malaila* oia i ike *ai,"* there (is the place) *in which* he saw. For further explanations see Part II.

ADVERBS.

§ 54. It does not enter into our plan to give a complete account of the adverbs in the language.

Any adjective or noun may be used as an adverb by being placed immediately after the verb.

The interrogative adverbs are all compounds of *hea,* as *auhea* and *mahea,* where? *pehea,* how? *nohea,* whence? *ihea,* whither? *ahea* and *inahea,* when? &c. Ahea refers to future and inahea to past time.

Questions which require "yes" or "no" for an answer, are asked by placing *anei* after the leading word in the sentence.

The Hawaiian has two negative adverbs, *aole* and *ole.* The former begins a sentence and is the general negative; the latter is a suffix, and may be added to almost any noun, adjective or verb in the language, like *un* and less in English. E. g., "hilahila *ole,*" shameless; "me ke kapa *ole,*" without clothes; "me ke noi *ole* mamua," without asking beforehand.

The following are the most common simple adverbs, which have not been mentioned already:

Ae, yes.
Paha, perhaps.
Ho'i, also, certainly.
Loa, very.
Iki, a little.
Pe, as.
Peia, thus.
Penei, in this way.
Pelá, in that way.
Wale, nearly, just so.
Wale, no, only.
Pu, together.

Aneane, almost.
Mai, nearly.
Pinepine, often.
Mau, continually, ever.
Oiai, and Oi, while.
Hou, again.
Anó, now.
Apopó, tomorrow.
Inehinei, yesterday.
Aia, there.
Eia, here.

Kainoa, I supposed, expressing surprise, as "Kainoa he oiaio, aole ka!" I thought it was true, but it is not.

COMPOUND PREPOSITIONS OR ADVERBS.

§ 55. A large class of words, expressing the relations of place, and which are really *nouns* with the article omitted, when preceded by either of the simple prepositions, serve as *adverbs* of place or time. When at the same time they are followed by a preposition, generally *o*, they serve as "compound prepositions."

E. g., "Ma (ka) loko," within, inside.
"Ma loko o ka hale," inside of the house.
"Ma waho," outside.
"Mawaho o ka hale," outside of the house.

The following is a list of the principal words of this class:

'O, yonder, from which are formed *ma'o, i'o,* &c.

Uka, inland.	Mua, before.
Hope, after, behind.	Muli, behind, after.
Kai, sea.	Kahi, where.
Lalo, below.	Waena, between.
Loko, inside.	Waho, outside.
Luna, above.	Laila, there.

Nei, here, which is *anei* after *i, ma,* or *mai,* as *ai nei, maanei.*

E. g., Mamua holo aku kekahi poe ilaila, formerly certain people sailed thither.

Nolaila, ua maopopo, therefore it is evident.
Noloko mai o ka moana, out of the ocean.
Haule ia iloko o ka lua, he fell into the pit.
Mamua aku nei, before this time.
Mahope o kona make ana, after his death.
Aole paha aina maanei, there was perhaps no land here.
Pii aku la lakou iluna, they ascended upward.
Mailalo mai, from below.
Mawaena o na mauna, among the mountains.
Aole au e hele iuka, I will not go inland.
Ma'o aku o ka hale, beyond the house.
E iho i kai, descend to the sea.
Ma kahi e ku ai na moku, at the place where ships anchor.

CONJUNCTIONS.

§ 56. These are few and simple. The principal conjunctions are as follows:

A, *and.* When it connects nouns, it always takes the preposition *me* after it, as *a me.*

A, long, also means *until, as far as, when,* and *when,* before verbs.

Aká, *but,* a strong adversative.

I, *that, in order that,* denoting purpose.

Ina, *if,* sometimes repeated again in the conclusion of a conditional sentence like "then."

I, *if,* a shorter form of *ina.*

I ole e. *if not,* or *in order that not.*

O, *lest.*

Ho'i, *also.*

Ke, *provided that,* used with a present or future meaning.

Nae, *however, yet.*

No ka mea, *because.*

For Examples See Part II.

INTERJECTIONS.

§ 57. Under this head may be mentioned the following:

E! O, used as a vocative sign, and in calling.

Ea! to call attention, as Hear!

Auwe! Alas! especially used in wailing.

Ka! and Káhahá! used to express surprise or disappointment.

Kahuhú! expressing strong disapproval.

Iná! O that, would that, and also Go to! Come on!

Hele pelá! Begone!

FORMATION OF WORDS.

§ 58. Most of the roots in Hawaiian as well as in the other Malayo-Polynesian languages are dissyllabic. A great many words are formed from others by doubling either the first or second or both syllables of the root. This reduplication, which is common to nouns, adjectives and verbs, expresses the idea of plurality, intensity or repetition.

Other derivative words are formed by prefixing some formative syllable as *pa, ka, ha, na, ma,* and *ki, po, pu,* &c. For the meaning of these formative syllables see Andrews' Dictionary. The verbal noun in *ana* has been mentioned above in section 49. It expresses the *action* signified by the verb. Other verbal nouns are formed by suffixing *na,* which more often refers to the result or the means of the action, than to the action itself. E. g., *hakina,* a broken piece, a fraction, from *haki,* to break; *mokuna,* a dividing line, from *moku,* to be broken or cut; *haawina,* a gift, from *haawi,* to give; *huina,* an angle, a junction, from *hui,* to unite, &c. Some of these forms are peculiar, as *komohana,* the west, from *komo,* to enter, or sink into, i. e. the going down of the sun; and *kulana,* a place where many things stand together, as a village, &c., from *ku,* to stand.

PART II.

An Outline of Hawaiian Syntax.

INTRODUCTORY REMARKS.

§ 1. SYNTAX, is defined to be that branch of grammar which treats of the construction of sentences. The Syntax, then, of a language like the Hawaiian, which has no inflections whatever, must chiefly relate to the arrangement of its words. It will not follow the methods of European grammars, nor will it have any use for the terms *"agreement"* or *"government."*

In such a language the structure of sentences must necessarily be *loose* rather than *compact.* In a highly cultivated language, such as the Greek, each period forms a symmetrical whole, with its beginning, middle and end, in which the relations of all the subordinate parts to the whole, and to each other, are clearly indicated, so that the words form a compact whole as well as the thought they express.

But a language which has not until lately been reduced to writing, or employed in carrying on consecutive trains of thought, must necessarily be wanting in means to express the connection and mutual dependence of its ideas. It will delight in short sentences, and will prefer to make its clauses *coordinate* rather than *subordinate,* and to keep them *distinct* rather than to incorporate them into the sentence as essential parts of it. Hence our principal task will be the analysis of simple sentences.

§ 2. Two ideas which pervade the language, and have great influence on its syntax, are (1) the distinction between living and inanimate things, and (2) that between transitive verbs on the one hand; and intransitive or passive ones on the other. Add to this the extensive use of the Possessive construction, so characteristic of all the Polynesian languages.

§ 3. In this as well as its cognate languages, most words may be used either as nouns, adjectives, verbs or adverbs, their meaning being indicated by their position in the sentence, and by the accompanying particles.

§ 4. The Hawaiian language has remarkable flexibility. Any one of its sentences may be cast in quite a variety of forms, all conveying different shades of meaning. The general principle of arrangement is that the emphatic word is to be placed at or near the beginning of the sentence. E. g.,

Ke haawi aku nei au i keia ia oe—I *give* this to you.
Owau ke haawi aku nei i keia ia oe—*I* give this to you.
O keia ka'u e haawi aku nei ia oe—I give *this* to you.
O oe ka mea a'u e haawi aku nei i keia—I give this to *you*.
Na'u keia e haawi aku nei ia oe—*I* give this to you.

SIMPLE SENTENCES.

§ 5. The following general principles are taken for granted :

Every proposition consists of two essential elements, the *subject* and the *predicate*. There are three subordinate elements, the *object,* the *adjective* element, and the *adverbial* element. Each of these five elements may consist of a single word, a phrase or a clause.

THE SUBJECT.

§ 6. *The Subject must follow its Predicate.*

This is the general rule. Exceptions to it, whether real or apparent; will be noticed below.

EXAMPLES.

1. Ua hele mai nei *au*—I have come here.
2. Ke uwe nei ke *keiki*—The child cries.
3. He aihue *ia*—He is a thief.

§ 7. The name of a *Person,* when in the *nominative* case, is regularly preceded by the "O emphatic."

EXAMPLES.

1. He alii mana o Kamehameha—Kamehameha was a powerful chief.
2. Make o Kahekili ma Oahu—Kahekili died on Oahu.
3. Holo aku la o Lono—Captain Cook sailed away.

NEGATIVE SENTENCES.

§ 8. In negative sentences, when the subject is a Pronoun, and sometimes when it is a proper name, it stands immediately after "aole," and before the predicate. If this latter is a verb or adjective, it generally takes the prefix "*i*" before it, or "*e*" if the time is future.

1. Aole au e hana hou i kau hana—I will not do your work again.
2. Aole au i pupule—I am not crazy.
3. Aole ia he mea e hilahila ai—That is not a thing to be ashamed of.

EMPHATIC ADVERBIAL PHRASES.

§ 9. Whenever an adverb or adverbial phrase, expressing time, place, cause or manner, stands for emphasis at the *beginning* of the sentence, the subject, if it be a *Pronoun,* precedes the verb. In sentences of this kind the verb is generally followed by the relative particle *ai,* of which more hereafter.

1. Malaila kaua e noho ai—It is *there* that we will dwell.
2. Pela no wau e hiki aku ai—That is the way that I will come.

Compare "Mahea oe e hele ai?"—Where are you going? and "E hele ana oe mahea?"

Note:—We have received the following acute suggestions from an accomplished Hawaiian scholar. "I imagine," says he, "that sections 8th and 9th are not *exceptions* to section 6th. The 'aole,' and the adverb or adverbial phrase are the *true predicates,* and the verb following with its adjuncts is *an infinitive* used adverbially, i. e., showing *how far* or in *what respect* the negation, or the circumstances of time, cause, &c., are predicated of the subject."

NOMINATIVE ABSOLUTE.

§ 10. The construction called *nominative absolute* in European grammars, is very common in Hawaiian. The subject in this construction is always preceded by the "O emphatic," and is represented by a pronoun after the predicate. This pronoun, "ia," is sometimes omitted, leaving the sentence incomplete. The construction just described is to be used whenever a sentence would begin with "as to" or "in respect to," &c.; in English; or when the subject is to be rendered prominent or emphatic; or when the subject is a phrase of some length.

1. O ka honua nei, he mea poepoe no ia—The earth here, it is a round thing.

2. O kona ma'i ana, o kona make no ia—Her sickness,
    that was (the cause of) her death.
3. O ka pono no ia, o ka noho na'auao—That is the
    right (thing), the living wisely.

ATTRIBUTE OR ADJECTIVE ELEMENT.

APPOSITION.

§ 11. Nouns in apposition follow the nouns which they
limit.   (1) If the leading noun is preceded by a preposition, this preposition is generally repeated before the noun
in apposition. (2) If, however, the noun in apposition be a
Proper Name, it may have either the "O emphatic" or the
repeated preposition before it.

EXAMPLES.

1. I ke kau ia Kalaniopuu i ke alii nui—In the time of
    Kalaniopuu, the great chief.
2. Kena ae la oia i kona kaikaina, o Haiao—He sent his
    younger brother, Haiao.

ATTRIBUTIVE ADJECTIVES.

§ 12. *An Attributive Adjective follows its Noun.* An adjective is called an attributive, when the quality, which it
expresses, is *assumed* or taken for granted, and not predicated of the subject. It is then a mere accessory or modi-
fier of the noun to which it belongs.

One noun may have two or more adjectives qualifying it.

EXAMPLES.

1. Ka palapala hemolele—The Holy Scriptures.
2. He poe liilii, nawaliwali, naaupo makou—We are a
    small, weak, ignorant company.

§ 13. Certain *limiting* adjectives, including the articles,
possessive, demonstrative and indefinite pronouns, and the
plural signs, *precede* their nouns. The plural signs are or
were originally nouns qualified by the following word, as

Ka poe bipi—the herd (of) cattle.

Keia mau hale—these houses.

Ko'u iio—my horse.

NUMERALS.

§ 14. Numerals generally *precede* their nouns. This is explained by the fact that they are really collective nouns like

"a myriad," "a decade," &c. But if they are *defined* by an article, or adjective pronoun, or noun preceded by the possessive *ko* or *ka,* then the numeral *follows.*

EXAMPLES.

Compare *"Elua kumu,"* two teachers, and
"Na haole elua," the two foreigners,
"Ehiku hale kula," seven school houses, and
"He mau hale kula eha," four school houses.

REMARK.—Ordinal numbers are generally followed by the preposition o between them and the nouns they qualify.

E. g. 1. I ke kolu o ka makahiki—In the third year; lit., in the third of the year.
    2. Ka mua o ka hale—the first house.
    3. Ka umi o ka hora—the tenth hour.

§ 15. The first nine numbers take the prefix *a* or *e,* while the round numbers from ten upwards, inclusive, take the article "he" or a numeral before them. See Part I, Section 31.

EXAMPLES.

"He umi," "he kanaha kanaka," "elua haneri."

REMARK.—"Nui," when it means "many" takes "he" before it, as if it were a collective noun, like the higher numerals.

EXAMPLES.

1. Hele mai na kanaka, *he* nui wale—there came *a great many* men.
2. But, "hele mai na kanaka nui loa" would mean "there came *very large* men."

ADJECTIVES USED AS NOUNS AND VICE VERSA.

§ 16. Any adjective may be used as an abstract noun by prefixing the definite article. On the other hand, any noun immediately following another has the force of an adjective.

EXAMPLES.

1. "Pono" means right, just, "ka pono," justice, &c.
2. He hana *kamalii* no ia, that is *childish* work.

REMARK.—In this way we explain the use of "mea" with a following noun to denote *owner* or possessor. Thus *"mea* aina" means owner of land. Here *"aina"* is an adjective qualifying "mea," person.

USE OF THE ARTICLES.

INDEFINITE ARTICLE.

§ 17.   This subject properly belongs to another branch of
grammar.   The indefinite article "he" is used chiefly with
the predicate of a sentence.   It is *never* used with the
object of a preposition.   When a noun used in an indefinite
sense is the object of a verb, the article is commonly omitted.
This is especially the case after *lilo* and other *verbs* signifying to change, appoint, constitute, &c., and before *"mea"* in
the sense of "cause" or "means" after *"i"* denoting purpose.
Often, when "some" or "a certain" might be substituted for
"a," *"kekahi"* takes its place.

EXAMPLES.

1. Nonoi aku la ia i la'au—He asked for medicine.
2. Haawi o Kamehameha i a'ahu hulu manu—Kamehameha gave a robe of birds' feathers.
3. E lilo i koa—To become a soldier.
4. Hoonoho oia i kekahi keiki i mea e hooino mai ia
   makou—He appointed a boy as a person to revile us.

DEFINITE ARTICLES.

§ 18.   The definite articles are generally used in the same
manner as in English.   They are also used in address, as "E
ka Lani e"—May it please your Majesty!   "Ka" is also
used before abstract and verbal nouns, where *"the"* would
not be used in English as "ka maika'i," goodness, &c.   It is
often used with a noun understood, which is generally *"mea,"*
"poe" or *"olelo."*

EXAMPLES.

1. Owau ka (mea) i olelo aku ia Boki—I am the (person
   who) said to Boki.
2. O lakou ka (poe) i ike—They were the (persons who)
   knew.

OMISSION OF THE DEFINITE ARTICLE.

§ 19.   The definite article is omitted before the words
kinohi and *kahakai;* as well as before *luna, lalo,* and other
words of that class, which are combined with simple prepositions to form compound prepositions and adverbs.   In the
following example the word *kahi,* is undoubtedly a contraction of *ka wahi.*   This supposition will account for its use
as an adverb of place.   The singular article *ka* is often used
in a collective sense when the plural would be employed in
English.

EXAMPLES.

1. I kinohi—In the beginning.
2. Ma kahakai—On the sea shore.
3. Ma luna o ka hale—Upon the house.
4. Ma kahi a makou i hele ai—In the place where we went.
5. Haawi mai ka haole ia lakou i ka hao—The foreigners gave them iron.

THE PREDICATE.

THE MODE OF EXPRESSING THE VERB "TO BE."

§ 20. In European languages, when the predicate is a noun or adjective, it is connected to the subject by the copula or verb "to be." In Hawaiian this verb is expressed by the arrangement of the words, aided in some cases by certain affirmative particles which are also used with other verbs.

§ 21. In order to explain the structure of Hawaiian sentences we must borrow from the science of Logic the distinction between common or general terms, and singular or individual terms. "The former can be affirmed of each of an indefinite number of things, the latter only of a single thing or collection of things."—*John Stuart Mill.*

A common noun may be a singular term, when defined or particularized by the accompanying words. Thus "the present king of England" and "this river" are individual or singular terms.

§ 22. CASE I.—The simplest form of a proposition is that which affirms the existence of something. Here the substantive verb in European languages is both copula and predicate. In English the expletive "there" is prefixed to the verb, when as is generally the case, it is followed by a "general term." In common with most other languages Hawaiian has no word to express the abstract idea of existence. Sometimes the words "to live" or "to dwell" are substituted for it. When the subject is a common noun, and "there" would be prefixed in English, the indefinite article *"he,"* or a *numeral* precedes the noun in Hawaiian. Often the affirmative particle *"no"* is added, which is also subjoined to verbs to strengthen an assertion.

EXAMPLES.

1. He wai no—There is water.
2. He lua wai ma ua wahi la—There was a well in that place.

3. Elua wahi e noho ai ke alii—There are two places for the king to dwell in.

§ 23. CASE 2.—When the *predicate* is *indefinite,* i. e., a "general term," or when the subject is affirmed to belong to a *class,* then the predicate *precedes* with *he* before *it,* according to Section 6.

EXAMPLES.

1. He kaula o Mose—Moses was a prophet.
2. He aihue ke kanaka—The man is a thief.
3. He ali'i mana o Kamehameha—Kamehameha was a powerful chief.
4. He poe anaana lakou nei—They are sorcerers.

§ 24. CASE 3.—Another kind of preposition is that which affirms the *identity* of two objects or collections of objects. From the nature of the case, the subject and predicate must both be individual or "singular terms," i. e., they must either be pronouns, proper names, or common nouns *defined* by some limiting words.

In *all* these cases, the sentence *begins* with the "O emphatic." A. When the predicate is a *common noun,* thus rendered *definite,* the *subject* generally *precedes* the predicate, with the "O emphatic" prefixed to it.

EXAMPLES.

1. Owau no kou ali'i—I am your chief.
2. O lakou ka poe i kohoia—They are the persons elected.
3. Oia ka'u pule i ko'u wa pilikia—That was my prayer in my season of distress.
4. O ka make ka mea e maka'u ai—Death is the thing to be afraid of.
5. O Hawaii ka mokupuni nui—Hawaii is the largest island.
6. O oe no ka'u i kii mai nei—You are the person I have come here for.
7. O olua ke hele, o wau ke noho—You two are to go, I am to stay.

EXCEPTION.—In certain cases when the predicate is emphatic and especially when the subject is a pronoun of the third person, the predicate *precedes* with the "O emphatic" before it.

EXAMPLES.

Compare 1. Oia no ka hewa—*This* (particular thing) was wrong, and

2. O ka hewa no ia—That was the *wrong* (of it).
3. O ke kaua iho la no ia—War was the immediate result.

4. O ka pau aku la ia o ko lakou kamailio ana—That was the end of their conversation.
5. O ka mana'o keia o ke ali'i—This was the thought of the chief.
6. O ka'u make kamalii no keia—This is my dying in youth. i. e., I am about to die in my youth.
7. O ka hele keia o kakou?—Is this our going, i. e., Shall we go now?

B.—The simplest affirmation of identity is in answering the question, "Who is it?" as "it is I," "it is John," &c. In Hawaiian the "O emphatic" is always prefixed to the predicate in such sentences, and "no" often follows it.

EXAMPLES.

1. Owau no—It is I.
2. O Ioane no—It is John.

C.—When the predicate is a *Proper Name* it generally precedes the subject, with the "O emphatic" before it.

EXAMPLES.

1. O Umi oe—Thou art Umi.
2. O Mala kona inoa—His name is Mala.
3. O I ka inoa o keia kanaka—This man's name is I.

§. 25. CASE 4.—Sometimes that which forms the predicate in Hawaiian is an *adverb* or adverbial phrase, which specifies the mode or place of existence. In such propositions the subject is (1) in most cases a *definite* or "singular term" and *follows* the adverbial expression. When on the other hand, (2) the subject is *indefinite,* the expletive "there" is prefixed in English, and in Hawaiian the subject generally *precedes* the adverbial expression, as in case 1.

EXAMPLES.

1. Pela ma Nu'uhiwa—So it is at Nukuhiwa.
2. Eia ka mea maika'i—Here is the good thing; i. e., the best thing.
3. Aia no Amerika, ma ka hikina—Yonder is America on the east.
4. Malaila no ia—There he is.
5. He lunakanawai ma kekahi kulanakauhale—There was a judge in a certain city.
6. He moku koonei—There is a ship here.
7. He aihue maloko o ka hale—There is a thief in the house.

PREDICATE ADJECTIVE.

§ 26. CASE 5.—When the predicate is an *Adjective*, it is known to be a predicate and not an attributive, by its position *before* the noun, according to section 5.

(1.) It often takes *he* before it, in which case it seems to be construed as a *noun,* or "mea" may be supplied after the *he.*

(2.) In many cases it takes *"ua"* before it, in which case it seems to be construed as a verb.

(3.) Sometimes, again, it stands abruptly at the beginning of the sentence without any prefix.

EXAMPLES.

1. *He* poepoe ka honua—The earth is round.
2. *He mea* poepoe ka honua—The earth is a round thing; i. e., a globe.
3. Ua nui na moku i ili—Many were the ships stranded.
4. He nui na kānaka i make—Many were the people who died. See section 15, Remark.
5. Nani ka naaupo!—What folly!
6. Ua huhu ia—He is angry.

VERBS.

§ 27. When the predicate is a verb, it *precedes* its subject according to the general rule, except in the two cases mentioned in sections 7 and 8. The following is the order in which the verb and its adjuncts are placed.

1. The tense signs, as *i, ua, e,* &c.
2. The verb itself.
3. The qualifying adverb, as *mua, wale, ole,* &c
4. The passive sign *ia.*
5. The directives, as *aku, mai,* &c.
6. The locatives, *nei,* or *la,* or the particles *ana* or *ai.*
7. The strengthening particle *no.*
8. The subject.
9. The object or predicate-noun.

Of course the above mentioned elements are never all found together at once. Of the four particles in the 6th place, viz., *nei, la, ana* and *ai,* if one is used, the others are excluded, except in a few cases where *la* is expressed after *ana.* The subject is sometimes omitted in rapid or excited speaking.

EXAMPLES.

1. E hana mua ia aku ana no ke alanui.
2. Malaila i malama malu ia aku ai o Laieikawai.

VERBAL NOUNS.

§ 28. Any verb may be used as a noun by simply prefixing to it the article or other definitive.

EXAMPLES.

1. Kaumaha oia i *ka lawe* ukana—He was tired of carrying baggage.
2. Me *ka noi ole* mamua—Without asking beforehand.
3. E'e iho la oia me *kona hoouna* ole *ia*—She went on board without having been sent.
4. Loaa ia Noa ke *alohaia* mai imua o Iehova—Noah found grace before Jehovah.

§ 29. More frequently the verb, when used as a noun, takes after it the particle *ana,* which denotes *continuance.* This form is equivalent to the participial noun in *ing* in English, but is used much more extensively. Observe that in this case *ana* precedes the *directives,* instead of following them as it does with the verb or participle.

EXAMPLES.

Compare 1. "E holo mai ana ia"—"He is sailing hither," and "Kona holo ana mai"—His sailing hither.
2. Pela ko ka makai hai ana mai *ia'u*—Thus was the constable's telling me, i. e., "So the constable told me."

THE VERB AS AN ADJECTIVE.

§ 30. Any verb may be used as an adjective, according to the principle stated in section 3. E. g., "Aloha," as a verb, means "to love," as a noun "love," as an adjective "loving," or "affectionate." When the idea of time is superadded, the verbal adjective may be called a *Participle.* The two forms generally used as participles, are:
1. The form with *i* prefixed to it, called the *past participle,* and
2. The form with *e prefixed* and *ana* or sometimes *nei* or *la affixed,* which we call the *present* or more properly the *imperfect participle.*

The form with *ua* prefixed, and that with *ke* prefixed and *nei* or *la* affixed, are occasionally used as participles. Like other adjectives they always *follow* their nouns. As will be seen hereafter, they very often supply the place of a relative clause.

EXAMPLES.

1. O kekahi kanaka *e noho ana* ma Olualu—A certain man living at Olualu.

2. Ma ka aina *i haawiia* nona—On the land given to him.
3. Ka poe *i haule*—The persons fallen, or who fell.

§ 31. The nouns "mea," and "poe" are very often omitted after the definite article before the past participle. The words *ka i,* like the Tahitian *tei* have often been mistaken for a relative pronoun, and are often written together as one word.

EXAMPLES.

1. Owau *ka* (mea) *i* olelo aku ia Boki—I am the (person) who said to Boki.
2. Oia *ka i* hoike mai ia ia—He is the (person) who declared him.
3. O na kauwa *ka* (poe) *i* ike—The servants were the (persons) who knew.

NOTE.—This construction resembles the definitive participle in Greek, and the "relative participle" in Tamil.

§ 32. Another class of sentences, instead of *ka i,* have *ke* before the verb, which might be considered a verbal noun denoting the agent or doer. This *ke* is perhaps a contraction of *ka e.* The difference between it and *ka i* seems to be that *ka i* is used in a *past,* and *ke* generally in a *present* or *future* sense.

EXAMPLES.

1. O ka mea malama i ka oiaio, oia *ke hele* mai i ka malamalama—He who keeps the truth, he it is that comes to the light.
2. O olua *ke* hele, owau *ke* noho—You two are the ones to go, I to stay.
3. O ko makou hale *ke* hiolo—It is our house that falls.

THE INFINITIVE.

§ 33. The infinitive may be the *Subject* of a clause, especially when the predicate is the verb *hiki,* in the sense of "can," *"pono"* or some other adjective, or a noun or pronoun, preceded by the preposition *na.* After "hiki," and often after "pono," it takes *ke* and not *e* before it. It may well be questioned, however, whether this form is a real infinitive.

EXAMPLES.

1. He pono i na kamalii a pau *e makaala*—It is right for all children to beware.
2. Aole pono *ke haawi* i ka hana ia hai—It is not right to give the work to another.
3. Na Hoapili *e kukulu* i hale pule, &c.—It is for Hoapili (i. e., Hoapili's duty) to build a meeting house.

4. Ua hiki i keia kamalii ke heluhelu—This child can read, literally—"It has come to this child to read."

N. B.—This is the regular way of expressing *"can"* in Hawaiian.

§ 34. The infinitive is often the *Object* of a verb, especially of such as denote some action or state of the mind, and those of asking, commanding or teaching.

EXAMPLES.

1. Paipai na kumu ia lakou e ku paa—The teachers urged them to stand fast.
2. Ao aku la kela ia lakou e pai palapala—That person taught them to print books.
3. Makemake no wau e hele—I wished to go.

OBJECT.

§ 35. The object of the verb is preceded by the preposition *i* or *ia,* which serves as an *objective sign.* In Hebrew we find *"eth"* used in a similar manner before a definite object, and so the preposition *á* in Spanish is used before the object, when it denotes an animated being.

Some verbs govern *two objects,* one direct and the other indirect, as

1. E haawi mai oe i ke kala ia'u—Give thou the money to me.
2. E ao aku ia lakou i ka heluhelu—Teach them to read.

§ 36. The objective sign "i" is always omitted before *ia,"* "that," and sometimes before nouns, especially after *mai* or *ai* or a verb ending in *i.*

EXAMPLES.

1. E holo e ike *ia* moku haole—Go and see that foreign ship.
2. E lawe mai oia *ia* mau bipi—He will bring those cattle.

§ 37. Participles and participial nouns take the same construction after them as verbs.

EXAMPLES.

1. I ko'u ike ana *i* ka lakou hana—On my seeing their work.
2. Ka haawi ana mai *i* ke kanawai—The giving of the law.
3. Nui wale kou kokua ana *ia* makou—Great was your assistance to us.

PREDICATE NOUNS.

§ 38. A proper name in the predicate after "kapa," to *name*
or *call,* always takes the "O emphatic" before it. A common
noun in the same situation is generally preceded by *"he,"* even
when it would have the definite article before it in English.

EXAMPLES.

1. Ua kapaia kona inoa o Puhi—His name was called Puhi.
2. Kapa aku la oia i kona inoa o Umi—He called his name
   Umi.
3. Aole au e kapa aku ia oukou he poe kauwa—I will not
   call you servants.

§ 39. After verbs signifying to become, to change, to
choose, to appoint or constitute, the predicate-noun commonly
takes the preposition *i,* "into," before it, and drops the article.
This *i,* is the same word as the conjunction "i" used to express purpose, the *hei* or *kei* of the Southern groups. This is
especially frequent in the phrase *i mea,* &c.

EXAMPLES.

1. E lilo ia i alanui maikai, ke hanaia—It will become a
   good road, if it be worked.
2. E hoolilo au ia oe i kaula—I will make you a prophet.
3. Ua koho au ia Kahale i luna kanawai—I have chosen
   Kahale as judge.

ADVERBS.

§ 40. As has been stated in section 27, the simple adverbs
are placed immediately after the verb or other word which
they qualify. Accordingly they always come between the verb
itself and *ana* or the passive sign *ia.* Any adjective may thus
be used as an adverb. The compound adverbs, mentioned in
Part I, Section 55, generally stand at the beginning or end of
the clause. They are really nouns preceded by a preposition,
with the article omitted.

EXAMPLES.

1. E uku *maikai* ia ka mea nana ka waiwai—He shall be
   well rewarded who owns the property.
2. E kukulu *hale* ana ia—He is house-building.
3. Ua oo ke kurina i kanu *lalani* ia—The corn planted in
   rows is ripe.
4. *Ma mua* holo aku kekahi poe *ma laila—Formerly* certain persons sailed *there.*
5. Aole ia i hele aku *i waho*—He did not go out.

PREPOSITIONS.

§ 41. Prepositions precede the nouns to which they relate, as in English. When two nouns are in *apposition,* the preposition is generally repeated before the latter noun as was stated in Section 11. When two nouns are connected by *a me,* "and," a preposition which relates to both nouns, is expressed only before the first. The preposition is sometimes repeated, however, after the conjunction *a.* Prepositions are frequently separated from the following nouns by the article or other limiting adjectives mentioned in Section 3. What are called compound prepositions are really *nouns,* preceded by a preposition, with the article omitted, and followed generally by *o,* but sometimes by *i.* For the distinction between *a* and *o,* &c., see Part I, Section 15.

EXAMPLES.

1. Me ka moi, me ka mea kiekie—With the king, the exalted personage.
2. E kuai i ka waina a me ka waiu—Buy wine and milk.
3. Kau a'e la maua ma luna o na lio—We two mounted on the horses.
4. Pii a'e la oia iluna, i ka la'au—He climbed up into the tree.

ELLIPSIS.

§ 42. After a noun preceded by *ko* or *ka,* the limited noun is often *omitted.* Thus *ko* before the name of a country denotes the inhabitants of that country, in which case "poe" is understood.

EXAMPLES.

1. Ko ke ao nei—The (people) of this world.
2. Ko Hawaii nei—The (people) of Hawaii.
3. Ka ke Akua (olelo)—God's word.
4. Ka Iseraela (mau keiki)—The children of Israel.

THE POSSESSIVE CONSTRUCTION.

§ 43. The possessive construction is far more extensively used in Hawaiian than in most other languages, and helps to supply the want of a relative pronoun. The thing possessed, in Hawaiian, is very often a verbal noun or infinitive.

EXAMPLES.

1. Aole a'u lohe i kona ano—I have not heard about his character.
2. Aole o'u ike i ka lawaia—I don't know how to fish.
3. He huhu kona—He is angry; lit., "An anger is his."

THE VERB "TO HAVE."

§ 44.   The verb "to have" is expressed by the prepositions *a* or *o, ka* or *ko* before the name of the possessor in the predicate.   "I have a book" would be expressed thus: "A book is mine."

CASE 1.   In *affirmative* sentences it is expressed by the prepositions *ka* or *ko* before the name of the possessor, *following* the thing possessed.

EXAMPLES.

1.   He mana'o ko'u—I have a thought.
2.   He palapala kau—You have a book.
3.   He kunu anei kou—Have you a cold?
4.   He aina kona—He has a land.

CASE 2.   In *negative* prepositions it is expressed by the propositions *o* or *a* and the word denoting the *possessor,* when a *pronoun, precedes* the thing possessed.

EXAMPLES.

1.   Aole ana buke—He has no book.
2.   Aole a'u palapala—I have no book.
3.   Aole anei ou wahi barena?—Have you not a little bread?

NOTE—To get, receive or find, is expressed by "loaa," used as a passive or neuter verb.   E. g., "ua loaa mai ia'u ka palapala," I have received the letter.

ON THE USE OF NA.

§ 45.   The preposition *na* is often placed before the noun denoting the *agent,* when an active verb or clause is the subject, to express duty or agency emphatically.

Thus, *"Nana* no e hoakaka"—It is for *him* to explain.   It is often used thus at the beginning of a sentence to point out the subject more emphatically, than the other construction in which the subject is expressed after the verb.   E. g.. *"Nana* i hana ka lani."   "He it was that made the heavens;" literally, "It was his to have made the heavens."   In this example *Nana* is the predicate, and the clause "i hana ka lani" is the subject.   The pronoun *Nana* may refer to a *plural* as well as to a singular antecedent.

§ 46.   When the *object* of the following clause is a *pronoun,* it generally *precedes* the verb, without the objective sign, *i.*   (In this case the pronoun seems to be construed as the subject, and the following verb to be subjoined adverbially to define the mode or extent.)

E. g. 1. "Na ke aupuni *oukou* e uku mai"—It is for the government to reward you—literally, "you are for the government to reward."

2. Na'u no *ia* e hoouna mai—I will send him—literally, "He is for me to send."

3. O ke Akua *nana makou* e kiai nei—God who watches over us,—literally, "Whose we are to watch over."

This last important use of *nana* as a relative pronoun will be explained more fully in Sec. 54.

INTERROGATIVE SENTENCES.

§ 47. These are of two kinds:

1. Direct interrogative sentences, which require *yes* or *no* for an answer. Such questions are asked in Hawaiian by putting *anei* after the leading word in the sentence. Affirmative questions which expect the answer "yes" begin with *Aole anei*.

EXAMPLES.

1. He moku anei keia?—Is this a ship?
2. Aole anei he Akua kou?—Have you not a God?
3. Ua holo anei ia?—Has he sailed?
4. Ua puhi anei oia i ka pu?—Has he blown the horn?

§ 48. 2. Indirect interrogative sentences, which require a sentence for their answer, and which are asked by interrogative words. These interrogative words are of three kinds:

1. Interrogative pronouns, as *wai* or *aha*.
2. Interrogative adjectives, as *hea* or *ehia*, and
3. Interrogative adverbs, as *ahea, pehea, auhea,* &c., which are compounds of *hea.*

These interrogatives generally stand at the beginning or end of a sentence, and very rarely in the middle.

EXAMPLES.

1. Owai ka mea aina maanei?—Who is the owner of land here?
2. Ua lilo ka palapala ia wai?—The book has passed to whom?
3. Ua hopuia ka aihue e wai?—By whom has the thief been taken?
4. Ehia ou mau makahiki?—How old art thou?

§ 49. Interrogative pronouns are seldom the subject of a verb. They are used in the nominative case, when there is a noun in the predicate, and the verb "to be" would be used in English, i. e., in Case 3, Section 24. With other *verbs* the form preceded by *na* is used, as has been explained in Section 45. The *answer* to a question must always closely correspond to it in construction.

EXAMPLES.

1. Nawai oe i hana? Na ke Akua—Who made you? God.
2. Mahea oe e hele ai?—Where are you going? or E hele ana oe mahea?
3. No keaha oe i hana ai pela?—Why (literally, *for what*) are you doing so?
4. Heaha ka inoa o keia aina? O Kualoa. What is the name of this land? Ans. Kualoa.

COMPLEX AND COMPOUND SENTENCES.

§ 50. A compound sentence consists of two or more independent propositions connected together by conjunctions.

A complex sentence consists of a principal and one or more subordinate clauses. From what has been already stated, it is evident that Hawaiian sentences are generally *compound* rather than *complex,* and their clauses are apt to be *co-ordinate* rather than *subordinate.* What would form a long sentence in English, in Hawaiian is generally broken up into several independent propositions, but loosely connected with each other.

We will next take up the various kinds of dependent clauses in English, and show how they are expressed in Hawaiian.

THE DEPENDENT CLAUSE USED AS SUBJECT.

§ 51. In European languages a substantive clause is frequently the subject of a sentence. Thus in the sentence, "It is evident that the earth is round," the word "it" is really an expletive, and the subject is the whole clause, "that the earth is round."

In Hawaiian the dependent clause is often *abridged,* and expressed by a substantive or by a participial noun, or again it is subjoined without any connective as an independent proposition.

Thus the sentence given above, might be rendered, "The roundness of the earth is evident"—ua akaka ka poepoe ana o ka honua; or, "It is evident; the earth is round"—"Ua maopopo, he poepoe no ka honua."

RELATIVE OR ADJECTIVE CLAUSES.

§ 52. The use of a real relative pronoun is confined to the most perfect class of languages, viz., the inflected languages. A relative pronoun *incorporates* its clause into the sentence as a *subordinate* part, and as an *adjective* element, qualifying some noun or pronoun in it. This noun or pronoun to which it refers is called the *antecedent.* Such clauses are expressed in Hawaiian, either in an abridged form by means of *adjectives* or *participles,* or by the Possessive Construction, explained above, which last furnishes a clear and compact mode of rendering such clauses when they are *short.* When they are *long* or involved, they must be rendered in Hawaiian by independent propositions.

§ 53. REMARK.—Observe that when the antecedent of the relative is a pronoun of the third person, as in the phrases, "he who," "those who," &c., it is expressed in Hawaiian by the nouns "ka mea" for the singular, and "ka poe" for the plural.

§ 54. CASE I. *When the Relative is Subject of its Clause.*

A.—When the clause contains the copula "to be," the relative is wanting, and the clause is expressed by an adjective simply, or by a noun in apposition. Thus, "the man who is honest" = "the honest man." "Paul, who was an apostle" = "Paul, an apostle." "He that is holy, he that is true" = O ka mea hoano, ka mea oiaio.

B.—When the relative is the subject of a verb, the clause is often expressed by a participle. This is the regular construction when the verb is *intransitive* or *passive.* Thus, "the thing which was given" = the thing given—ka mea i haawiia.

E. g. 1. Ka poe i haule—The people who fell.
2. Ka poe e noho ana maluna o ke kuahiwi—They who dwell on the mountain.
3. He nui ka mea e ae i hanaia—Many were the other things which were done.

C.—The relative is expressed by *nana,* by the construction in Section 45, when the following verb is *active* and *intransitive,* and when the agent is a *person.* The tense signs are *i* in past time, and *e* in present or future time.

E. g. 1. Ka mea *nana* au i hoouna mai—He who sent me.
2. O Iuda *nana* ia i kumakaia—Judas who betrayed him.
3. O oe ke kanaka *nana* i aihue ko'u lio—You are the man who stole my horse.
4. O ke Akua *nana* e ike i na mea a pau—God who sees all things.

5. Aole o'u mea *nana* e hai mai, &c.—I had no one to tell me, &c.

§ 55. CASE 2. *When the Relative is Object of its Clause.*

What would be the *subject* of the clause in English, is put into the possessive form, i. e., preceded by the preposition *a* or *ka*, as if the antecedent were a thing possessed, and the verb is subjoined as with *nana*. The prefix preposition "ka" is used when the noun (generally *mea*) *follows* or is understood.

The relative particle *ai* always follows the verb, except when *nei, la,* or *ana* takes its place.

E. g. 1. "What I tell you"—"My thing to tell you"—Ka'u mea e hai aku *nei* ia oukou.

2. "The things which I saw—the things of me to have seen"—Na mea a'u i ike *ai*.

3. "This is what they saw—here is theirs to have seen"—Eai ka lakou i ike *ai*.

4. A tale which my mother told me—He kaao a ko'u makuahine i hai mai ai ia'u.

5. Ke kumu niu a maua i ae like ai—The coconut tree which we two agreed about.

§ 56. CASE 3. When the relative is in the *possessive case,* or *is governed by a preposition.*

A.—When it relates to a *person* it is expressed in Hawaiian by a *personal pronoun* in the same construction.

E. g. 1. O ka mea *ia ia ke ki*—He to whom the key belongs.

2. "E ke Akua mana loa, *me oe* e noho la ka uhane o ka poe i haalele i keia ao"—"Almighty God, *with whom* dwell the spirits of the departed."

3. "Ka mea *ma ona la* ia i hana ai i ka lani a me ka honua"—"The person by whom he made the heaven and the earth."

B.—When the relative refers to a *thing,* which is the *cause, means* or *instrument* "by which" any thing is or is done, the relative is generally expressed only by the particle *ai,* which *always* follows the verb in such clauses.

E. g. 1. Eia ka mea e make ai na kanaka—"This is the cause from which the people decrease."

2. Oia ke kumu i kaua ai lakou—That was the cause for which they fought.

3. Heaha kau mea i hiki mai ai—What is your reason for coming?

4. "Ka kaua mea i au mai *nei* (for *ai*) i keia mau kai ewalu"—"The reason for which we have sailed hither

over these eight seas," or "Our reason for sailing hither," &c.

C.—When the relative refers to a noun denoting the *time* or *place,* "in which" or "at which" any thing is or is done, the possessive construction explained in Section 55 is preferred when a *person* is the agent, and an *active* verb follows. In this case the preposition *a* is generally used before the noun denoting the agent, but sometimes *ko* especially when *wahi* follows. The verb is always followed by the relative particle *ai,* or *nei,* which sometimes takes its place. Often, however, and always when a *passive* verb follows, the construction given in the last paragraph (B) is preferred, the relative being expressed simply by *ai* after the verb.

E. g. 1. "At the time in which Captain Cook arrived— When Captain Cook arrived"—"I ka wa i ku mai o Lono."

2. "At Kona, the place where he lived"—Ma Kona kona wahi i noho ai.

3. "Ma ke alanui a makou i hele ai"—In the road in which we went.

4. "Ma kahi i hunaia 'i o Kaahumanu"—At the place where Kaahumanu was concealed.

5. I Waiapuka kahi i malama ia ai o Liloa—At Waiapuka where Liloa was kept.

6. Ka wa i make ai na 'lii ma Beritania—When the chiefs died in England.

7. Ma Laie kona wahi i hanau ai—At Laie, her birth place.

8. Ka aina a'u e noho *nei*—The land in which I dwell.

Observe that kahi = ka wahi.

ADVERBIAL CLAUSES.

Adverbial Clauses of Place.

§ 57. Most adverbial clauses of place are expressed in the manner explained in the last section. Some *noun* denoting *place* must be expressed, and connection of the clauses indicated by *ai.* Thus, "where," "whither" and "whence" are generally expressed by "kahi" or "wahi," &c., with "ai" after the following verb.

E. g. 1. The land *where* we journey—O ka aina kahi a maua e hele ai.

2. Whence I came—Ko'u wahi i hele mai ai.

3. Whither I go—Ko'u wahi e hele aku ai.

"Wherever"—"ma na wahi a pau a —— ai."

"*As far as*" is expressed by a circumlocution, as, e. g., "As far as the East is from the West"—E like me ka loihi mai ka hikina a i ke komohana.

Adverbial Clauses of Time.

§ 58. These clauses generally assume the forms given in Section 56, C. They are generally connected to the leading proposition by "when" or "while" in English. In Hawaiian some noun denoting time must be expressed, and the connection of the clauses indicated by the relative particle *ai*.

E. g. 1. I ka wa i make ai na 'lii—When the chiefs died.
2. I kona wa e maalo ae ana—While he passes by.

"Whenever" or *"As often as"* is expressed by "i na wa a pau a —— ai." E. g. "I na wa a pau a oukou e ai ai"—As often as ye eat." *"As long as"* is similarly expressed, as "i na la a pau a —— ai."

§ 59. A looser mode of connecting such clauses, when less precision is required, is by the conjunction *a* or *aia,* which is equivalent to "when," "and when," "until," &c.

E. g. 1. A hiki mai ia—When he arrives.
2. Aia ike aku oe i ka manu—When you see the bird.
3. A ahiahi iho—When it was evening.
4. A ao ka po—When it was morning.

§ 60. Another mode of rendering clauses connected by "while" or "when" is by prefixing the preposition *i* or *ia* to the subject, when it is a *person,* and placing after it a form of the verb, which *may* be considered as a participle. When the progressive form in *ana* follows, it is to be rendered by "while" with a verb; when the past participle, by "when," or "as soon as." In the latter case the verb is always followed by *ai.* This use of *ai* may *possibly* be explained by ellipsis as follows:

E. g. 1. "(I ka wa) ia ia i hiki ai iluna pono o Kalala"— As soon as he reached the summit of Kalala.
2. "Ia ia e noho ana malaila"—While he was sitting there.
3. "Ia lakou i ike aku ai ia ia"—As soon as they saw him.
4. "Ia'u e noho ana me oukou"—While I am with you.

Some Hawaiian scholars make the following distinction.

Ia ia e hele *ana aku*—While he was going.
Ia ia e hele *aku ana*—When he was about to go.

§ 61. A clause introduced by *"while"* in English, may also be rendered by a participial noun, preceded by a preposition, as "i ko'u hele ana 'ku"—"While I was going." (Lit. "in my going.") This is a very common construction.

Oiai is often used for "while," especially when the clause, in English, has for its predicate the verb "to be," followed by a

noun. Thus, Oiai ka la = "While it is day." Oiai ka malamalama me oukou = "While the light is yet with you." A
shorter form of the same is *oi*. E. g., "E hele i ka malamalama *oi* kau ke ea i ke kino."

§ 62. Clauses introduced by "before," "since," or "after,"
are expressed by the compound prepositions *mamua o* and
mahope o, followed by a *participial noun* as "Before I went"
= Mamua o ko'u hele ana aku;" "mamua o ka wa e ko ai"=
before it is accomplished. "Mahope iho o kona hiki ana
mai"—After he arrived.

§ 63. The use of *ai* in the sentences beginning with an
adverbial expression, spoken of in Section 9, may be account-
ed for from the analogy of relative clauses, by supposing an
ellipsis.
E. g., Thus, "malaila oia i ike ai"—That (is the place) *in
which* he saw.
"Pela no oia i malama aku ai ia lakou"—That's the way *in
which* he took care of them.
As was before stated, the subject, if a *pronoun,* generally
precedes the verb in such sentences, as "Pehea la *oukou* i ike
ai ia mea?"—How do you know that?

FINAL CLAUSES.

§ 64. Final clauses are those which denote a *purpose* or
motive. These are generally introduced by *i,* "that," "in
order that," *i ole e,* "that not," or *o,* "lest." Sometimes purpose is expressed by an infinitive followed by *ai,* which is
equivalent to "in order to," with the infinitive in English.
The particle *ai* sometimes occurs in final clauses introduced
by *i,* to bring out the idea of the "means" or "cause." It can
be rendered by "whereby" or "thereby," and explained by
substituting *i mea e* for *i.*
E. g. 1. "E hooikaika oe i na keiki i loaa 'i ka pono"—Ex-
hort the children *in order that* they may receive *good.*
    2. "Kua lakou i ka laau ala i pau ka aie"—They cut down
sandal-wood *in order that* the debt might be paid.
    3. "Aole laua i ai pu o pepehiia laua"—They two did not
eat together *lest* they should be killed.
    4. "Mai hele oe i ka lua Pele o make oe"—Do not go to
the Volcano, lest you die.

§ 65. CLAUSES WHICH EXPRESS CORRE-SPONDENCE OR COMPARISON.

The Hawaiian is very poor in means of expressing comparison. Such sentences must generally be broken up into

independent propositions. Clauses introduced by "as," in English, are expressed in Hawaiian by *like,* followed by a relative clause of the kind explained in Section 55.

E. g. 1. *"E like me ka'u* i olelo aku ai ia oukou"—As I told you, (lit., "like what I told you," or "like mine to have told you.")

2. *"E like me ka'u* i aloha ai ia oukou, pela oukou e aloha aku ai i kekahi i kekahi"—As I have loved you, so love ye one another.

Clauses introduced by "so—that," expressing a *consequence* are stated as independent propositions in Hawaiian. *"How,"* introducing a *dependent* clause, is expressed by a circumlocution, as follows: "You have heard how Abraham used to burn lambs on altars"—Ua ike oukou i ke ano o ka Aberahama ho'a ana i na hipa keiki maluna o na kuahu.

§ 66. CLAUSES WHICH EXPRESS A CAUSE OR REASON.

In English, such clauses are connected to the leading proposition by one of the conjunctions, "because," "since," "for," "as," &c. In Hawaiian they are either introduced by *no ka mea,* "because," or are expressed by the preposition *no* followed by a verbal noun.

E. g. 1. "No ka mea ua ike no oia i na mea a pau"— Because he knew all things.

2. "No ko lakou ike ana i na mea ana i hana 'i—For they knew the things which he did.

CONDITIONAL CLAUSES.

§ 67. In these the condition is introduced by *ina* "if," either alone or followed by the tense signs *i, e,* or *ua;* by *i,* a shorter form of *ina;* or by *ke,* "provided that," which is used of present or future time. The clause beginning with *ke,* generally is subjoined at the end of the sentence, while *i* or *ina* stand at the beginning. *"If not"* is expressed by putting *ole* after the verb, and *ina,* &c., before it, or by the phrases *i ole e* or *ke ole.* In a long sentence the conclusion is often marked by a second *ina,* equivalent to "then" in English.

E. g. 1. Ina i hele mai nei oe, *ina* ua ike—If you had come here, then you would have seen.

2. Ina i makemake mai oe ia mea, ina ua kii mai oe—If you had wanted this thing, then you would have come for it.

3. E maluhia lakou *ke* hiki mai—They shall be at peace if they come.

4. *A i hoi ole* mai, kaua no—And if he does not come, it is war.

OBJECTIVE CLAUSES.

§ 68. Objective clauses generally follow verbs which denote 1st, some act or state of the mind, or 2nd, a declaration or command. Such causes are introduced by "that" in English. In Hawaiian they are often expressed by the infinitive after the verbs mentioned in Section 34. Often, however, especially after verbs of saying, or declaring, they stand without any connecting particle before them. There is no distinction then in Hawaiian Grammar between direct and indirect quotation.

SPECIMENS OF HAWAIIAN SENTENCES ANALYZED.

§ 69. The first passage we have selected is from the account of the Temptation of Christ, (Matt. iv. 1.)

```
              1                    2   3  4
V. 1.  Alaila, alakaiia 'ku la o Iesu e ka Uhane i ka
       Then   was led away          Jesus by the Spirit to the

       5            6              2  7
waonahele, e hoowalewaleia 'ku ai e ka Diabolo
wilderness to    be tempted         by the Devil.
```

Then was Jesus led up of the Spirit into the wilderness to be tempted by the Devil.

NOTES 1. *Alakaiia* is compounded of *ala*, way, the Javanese *jalan*, and *ka'i* to lead; *ia* is the Passive sign. 2. The initial *a* of the verbal directive *aku*, is contracted with the final one of the preceding word. 3. *La* here is the sign of past time, (See Part I, § 48 and § 52.) 4. *O* here is the sign of the nominative with proper names. Part I, § 26. 5. *Waonahele* is compounded of *wao*, an uninhabited place, and *nahele*, overgrown with bushes, &c. 6. *Hoowalewaleia* is compounded of *ho'o*, the causative prefix. (See Part I, § 51), *walewale*, to deceive, and *ia* the Passive ending. 7. *Ai* is the relative particle, and with the preceding *e* serves to express the idea of purpose, "in order to," (See Part II, § 64).

         I   2   3   4

V. 2.   Hookeai   iho   la ia i   hookahi   kanaha la,
         Fasted   *thereupon*   *he for*   *one*   *forty days*

  5   6   2   7

a me   na   po   he   kanaha, a   mahope   iho,   pololi
and   *the*   *nights*   *a*   *forty*   *and afterwards*   *hungry*

     2   3

   iho   la   ia.
accordingly (was) he.

And when he had fasted forty days and nights, he was afterwards a hungered.

NOTES. 1. *Hookeai* is compounded of *hooke,* to abstain, and *ai,* food. *Hooke* again is compounded of *ho'o,* the causative prefix, and *ke,* to elbow, to push away. 2. *Iho* is a directive particle. (See Part I, § 52.) It expresses here the idea of *sequence,* like "thereupon," "immediately after," "accordingly." 3. *La* denotes past time as in V. 1. 4. *Ho'o-kahi* is compounded of *kahi,* the numeral, one, and the prefix *ho'o,* and expresses with precision, "one," "only one." 5. *A me,* and, is used to connect nouns, *a* to connect verbs. 6. The plural definite article. 7. On the structure of this sentence, see Part II, § 26. The position of the adjective shows that it is predicated of the subject. Or, "pololi" may be constructed as a verb, "he hungered," which view is confirmed by the use of the verbal particles *iho* and *la* after it.

            I   2

V. 3.   A   hiki   aku ka   hoowalewale   i ona
       And when   *came*   *forth the*   *tempter*   *to him*

           3   4   5   6 7

la   i   aku   la   ia, Ina o ke   Keiki   oe   a   ke   Akua.
there said forth   *he*   *if*   *the*   *son*   *thou of the*   *God*

8   9

e   i   mai   oe   i   keia mau pohaku   i
  speak hither   *thou*   *to*   *these*   *stones*   *that (they)*

    10

  lilo   i   berena.
become to bread.

And when the tempter came to him he said, If thou be the Son of God, command that these stones be made bread.

NOTES. 1. *A* long at the beginning of a clause often means "when," "and when," "until." 2. For the form *i ona la,* "to him," see Part I, § 20 and § 38. 3. *I* here is the verb, to say, in the past tense. 4. *La* signifies past time as usual. 5. *O* here is the article *o*, used to render the following noun emphatic, in a clause affirming the *identity* of two things. See Part II, § 24. 6. For the distinction between *a* and *o* see Part I, § 15. 7. For the use of the form *ke* rather than *ka,* see Part I, § 24. 8. *E* is the sign of the imperative. 9. *Mau* is the sign of the plural. 10. On this use of *i* see Part II, § 39.

			1	2				3
V. 4.	Olelo	mai	la o	Iesu,	i	mai	la,	Ua
	Spake	*hither*		*Jesus,*	*said*	*hither*		*(It) has*

4	5				6			
palapalaia,	Aole	e	ola	ke	kanaka	i	ka	berena
been written	*Not*	*shall*	*live*	*the*	*man*	*by*	*the*	*bread*

7					8			
wale	no,	aka,	ma	na	mea	a	pau	mai ka waha
alone		*but*	*by*	*the*	*things*		*all*	*from the mouth*

9
mai o ke Akua.
hither of the God.

But he answered and said, It is written, Man shall not live by bread alone, but by every word that proceedeth out of the mouth of God.

NOTES. 1. *La* is the sign of the past time. 2. *O* is the article *o*, used with proper names in the nominative, Part II, § 7. 3. *Ua* is the sign of the perfect tense. 4. *Palapala* is the verb, to write, and *ia* is the passive sign. 5. *E* is the sign of the future. 6. *I* means "by" after an intransitive verb or adjective, but *e* is used after a passive verb. 7. *No* is a strengthening particle, Part I, § 49, and generally accompanies *wale,* which signifies "only," "alone." 8. *A pau,* "all," originally meant "until done," "completed." 9. On the repetition of *mai,* see Part I, § 14.

§ 70. The next passage is from the romance of Laieikawai, Page 13.

1	2		3				
I. Iloko	o ko	Laieikawai	mau	la	ma	Waiapuka,	ua
During		*Laieikawai's*		*days*	*at*	*Waiapuka*	*was*

4		5					
noomauia	ka	pio	ana	o	ke	anuenue ma	kela
continued	*the*	*arch-*	*ing*	*of*	*the*	*rainbow at*	*that*

	1				6		
wahi;	iloko	o	ka	manawa	ua	a	me ka
place	*in*		*the*	*time*	*rainy*	*and*	*the*

malie,   i ka   po   me ke ao;   aka,   aole
fair weather   in the night   and the day   but   not

     7   8

nae i hoomaopopo na   mea   a pau i ke   ano   o
yet   understood   the persons   all   the   nature   of

                             4

keia anuenue; aka, ua   hoomauia keia mau   hoailona
this   rainbow   but   were   continued   these   signs

 6   7   9   10 11   3
alii ma na wahi   i   malamaia '¡   ua   mau
chief   at the places (where) were guarded   these

mahoe nei.
twins.

In the days when Laieikawai was at Waiapuka, the arching
of the rainbow was continued at that place in rainy weather
and in fair weather, by night and by day; but yet all persons
did not understand the nature of this rainbow; but these
tokens (of a) chief were continued in the places where these
twins were guarded.

NOTES. 1. *Iloko o* is a compound preposition like inside of
in English. (Part I, §55). 2. *Ko* is the prefix preposition,
"of," on which see Part I, §18. 3. *Mau* is a sign of the
plural. 4. *Hoo-mau-ia. Mau* means continual, *ho'o* is the
causative, and *ia* the passive sign. 5. *Pio ana* is a sort of
participial noun. Part II, §29. 6. The nouns *ua* and *alii* are
used here as adjectives. 7. *I* here is the sign of the past
tense. 8. *I* is the sign of the objective case. 9. In *malamaia, ia* is the passive sign. 10. The initial *a* of the particle
ai is absorbed in the final *a* of the preceding word. The relative *ai* here refers back to *wahi,* like "where" in English.
Part I, §53. 11. Ua nei taken together mean *"these."* Part
I, §43.

                      1   2   3
II. I kekahi manawa ia Halaaniani e kaahele ana ia
    On a certain   time   to Halaaniani   travel-   ing

Kauai a   puni   ma kona   ano   makaula   nui
Kauai   around   in his character (as) prophet   great

              4   5   6   7   8
no Kauai, a   ia ia i hiki   ai iluna pono o Kalalea,
of Kauai and   to him   arrived   upon   right Kalalea

              9   10
ike mai   la oia i ka   pio a   keia anuenue i Oahu
saw hither then he   the arch of this   rainbow on Oahu

11
nei; noho   iho   la oia   malaila he iwakalua   la   i
here dwelt accordingly   he   there   a twenty   day   as a

                   12 13   15   14
kumu   e   ike   maopopo   ia 'i   ke   ano   o   kana
means to seen   clearly   be by which the   nature of   his

mea e ike nei.
thing to see here.

On a certain time while Halaaniani was traveling around Kauai, in his character (as) great prophet of Kauai, when he arrived at the very summit of Kalalea, he saw the arch of this rainbow on Oahu here; he accordingly dwelt there twenty days, in order to discern more clearly the nature of what he saw.

NOTES. 1. *Ia* here is a preposition, and *e kaahele ana* the present participle. On this mode of expressing "while" in English, see Part II, § 60. 2. *Kaahele ana,* is compounded of *kaa,* to roll, *hele,* to go, and *ana,* which denotes continuance, and is equivalent to *"-ing"* in English. It means then "traveling around," "making the tour of." 3. *Ia* here is the sign of the objective case. 4. *Ia ia,* the first *ia* is the preposition, and the second the pronoun, Part I, § 38. The construction is similar to that explained in Note 1. See Part II, § 60. 5. *I* is the sign of past time. 6. *Ai* is the relative particle. 7. *I luna o,* is a compound preposition, like "on top of" in English. Part I, § 55. 8. *Pono* is an adverb, "right," "exactly," and qualifies *i luna.* 9. *La* serves as sign of past time. 10. *I* is sign of the objective case, like *ia,* in Note 3. 11. *I* here denotes purpose. It means literally, "as a means, whereby might be discerned," &c. 12. *Ia* is the passive sign of *ike* separated from it by the adverb *maopopo.* 13. *Ai* has dropped its *a.* It may be rendered "whereby," and refers to *kumu,* Part II, § 56 B. 14. See Part II, § 55. *Nei* takes the place of *ai* after the verb. 15. The subject of "ike maopopo ia" is "ke ano," &c.

In conclusion, the author would express his obligations to Judge Andrews' Hawaiian Grammar, for many of the *examples* quoted in this little work.

INDEX.

Other TUT BOOKS available:

A HISTORY OF JAPANESE LITERATURE *by W. G. Aston*

HISTORICAL AND GEOGRAPHICAL DICTIONARY OF JAPAN *by E. Papinot*

HOMEMADE ICE CREAM AND SHERBERT *by Sheila MacNiven Cameron*

HOW TO READ CHARACTER: A New Illustrated Handbook of Phrenology and Physiognomy, for Students and Examiners *by Samuel R. Wells*

IN GHOSTLY JAPAN *by Lafcadio Hearn*

INDIAN RIBALDRY *by Randor Guy*

JAPAN: An Attempt at Interpretation *by Lafcadio Hearn*

THE JAPANESE ABACUS *by Takashi Kojima*

THE JAPANESE ARE LIKE THAT *by Ichiro Kawasaki*

JAPANESE ETIQUETTE: An Introduction *by the World Fellowship Committee of the Tokyo Y.W.C.A.*

THE JAPANESE FAIRY BOOK *compiled by Yei Theodora Ozaki*

JAPANESE FOLK-PLAYS: The Ink-Smeared Lady and Other Kyogen *translated by Shio Sakanishi*

JAPANESE FOOD AND COOKING *by Stuart Griffin*

JAPANESE HOMES AND THIER SURROUNDINGS *by Edward S. Morse*

A JAPANESE MISCELLANY *by Lafcadio Hearn*

JAPANESE RECIPES *by Tatsuji Tada*

JAPANESE TALES OF MYSTERY & IMAGINATION *by Edogawa Rampo; translated by James B. Harris*

JAPANESE THINGS: Being Notes on Various Subjects Connected with Japan *by Basil Hall Chamberlain*

THE JOKE'S ON JUDO *by Donn Draeger and Ken Tremayne*

THE KABUKI HANDBOOK *by Aubrey S. Halford and Giovanna M. Halford*

KAPPA *by Ryūnosuke Akutagawa; translated by Geoffrey Bownas*

KOKORO: Hints and Echoes of Japanese Inner Life *by Lafcadio Hearn*

KOREAN FOLK TALES *by Im Bang and Yi Ryuk; translated by James S. Gale*

KOTTŌ: Being Japanese Curios, with Sundry Cobwebs *by Lafcadio Hearn*

KWAIDAN: Stories and Studies of Strange Things *by Lafcadio Hearn*

LET'S STUDY JAPANESE *by Jun Maeda*

THE LIFE OF BUDDHA *by A. Ferdinand Herold*

MODERN JAPANESE PRINTS: A Contemporary Selection *edited by Yuji Abe*

NIHONGI: Chronicles of Japan from the Earliest Times to A.D. 697 *by W. G. Aston*

Please order from your bookstore or write directly to:

CHARLES E. TUTTLE CO., INC.
Suido 1-chome, 2–6, Bunkyo-ku, Tokyo 112

or:

CHARLES E. TUTTLE CO., INC.
Rutland, Vermont 05701 U.S.A.